The Catullian Influence in English Lyric Poetry,

Circa 1600-1650

THE UNIVERSITY OF MISSOURI STUDIES
Volume III Number 3

The Catullian Influence in English Lyric Poetry,

Circa 1600-1650

by John Bernard Emperor

OCTAGON BOOKS

A DIVISION OF FARRAR, STRAUS AND GIROUX

New York   1973

Originally published in 1928

Reprinted 1973
by special arrangement with the University of Missouri Press

OCTAGON BOOKS
A DIVISION OF FARRAR, STRAUS & GIROUX, INC.
19 Union Square West
New York, N. Y. 10003

LIBRARY OF CONGRESS CATALOG CARD NUMBER: 78-159183
ISBN 0-374-92589-5

PREFATORY NOTE

The study which follows is, in a certain sense, at once incomplete and more than complete; incomplete, in that it is, manifestly and necessarily, not the result of an examination of *all* the English lyric poetry of the period with which it deals; more than complete, in that I have, in dealing with certain of the authors of my study, felt called upon, for the sake of thoroughness, to include quotations, not merely from their non-lyrical poems, but from their prose. For the latter procedure, which, if it be a fault at all, is a fault near allied to virtue, I make no apology. For the first, I have but to say that I feel that, in the thirty-seven poets dealt with in this study, I number all the notable and most of the known poets of the period of my investigation. Omissions there are, to be sure, but no poet, I say with a certain confidence, has been omitted whom it would be at all profitable to include.

I am indebted to Professor Martin Wright Sampson of Cornell University for his valuable assistance during the preparation of this study.

J. B. E.

ERRATA

Page 44 In (4) for *comparier* read *compararier*.
Page 47 In (2) for *comparier* read *compararier*.
Page 55 In (13) for *comparier* read *compararier*.
Page 76 and 77 For *Brittannia's Pastorals* read throughout *Britannia's Pastorals*.
Page 101 For *fort mediocres* read *fort médiocres*.
Page 126 For note 2 see Page 127.

TABLE OF CONTENTS

THE CATULLIAN INFLUENCE IN
ENGLISH LYRIC POETRY, CIRCA 1600-1650

John Bernard Emperor

INTRODUCTION

THE CHARACTERISTICS OF CATULLUS'S POETRY

We may well begin our study of the influence of Catullus upon one of the very greatest periods of English lyric poetry by a short discussion of the characteristics of the Latin poet, as we can gather them from his comparatively slender body of verse. It will then be for us to consider what in these qualities of Catullus would make his poetry attractive, either as an inspiration or as a source for actual imitation or translation, to the English poets of the seventeenth century.

First of all, Catullus is one of the supreme poets of love, the greatest singer of ardent passion. Compared with him, the other great erotic poets in Latin literature are feeble triflers working on a theme they do not more than half comprehend. Preëminently, then, Catullus is the poet of burning passion, of overmastering love, and it is as a poet of love that he will appear most often in this study. The distinguishing marks of good love poetry are simplicity and a certain fiery earnestness, and these are, in a superlative degree, the qualities of Catullus. The most famous criticism of the poet is that of the pious Fénelon; in two words he has accounted for the greatness of the lover of Lesbia:

> Catulle, qu'on ne peut nommer sans avoir horreur de ses obscenités, est au comble de la perfection pour une *simplicité passionnée:*
> Odi et amo. Quare id faciam fortasse requiris:
> Nescio, sed fieri sentio et excrucior.
> Combien Ovide et Martial, avec leurs traits ingénieux et façonnés, sont ils au dessoux de ces paroles negligées, où le coeur saisi parle seul dans un espèce de désespoir.[1]

The poets who followed Catullus recognized and imitated the transcendent genius of the fiery young Veronese, and it was primarily as a love poet that they knew and valued him. Munro puts this part of Catullus's influence briefly and well:

> That, owing to temporary and social causes, Horace had a certain jealousy of Catullus there can be no doubt, tho' he is at the same time his frequent imitator. Virgil has studied him much, as is shown in his very earliest poems and in his *Aeneid*; while Ovid, the most candid and unenvious of men, sets no bounds to his admiration. . . . To Martial, who belonged to the last age in which Roman literary judgment was of much value, Catullus was supreme. Martial, obeying the irreversible verdict of his countrymen, freely acknowledged Virgil as sovereign of Latin poetry, yet he seems to worship him at a distance, and his first and second loves, his Delia and his Nemesis, are Catullus and Ovid.[2]

It will be seen, in this study, that a part of the influence of Catullus upon the poets of the seventeenth century was exercised, as it were, through intermediaries, through Latin poets who were themselves imitators of Catullus, and whose imitations may

---

1 Quoted in Munro's *Criticisms and Elucidations of Catullus*, p. 233.
2 Munro, *op. cit.*, p. 232.

have been the inspiration or model for a Jacobean or Caroline poet, rather than the Catullian original itself.[3]

Secondly, Catullus is characterized by a deep strain of tender melancholy. Tennyson's beautiful lines on Sirmio are justly famous:

> There beneath the Roman ruin where the purple flowers grow,
> Comes that "Ave atque Vale" of the poet's hopeless woe,
> Tenderest of Roman poets nineteen hundred years ago.[4]

This strain of sadness is to be found in much of the love poetry, especially in the poems of doubt, of sorrow, and of detestation; it appears most plainly and least pleasingly in those few poems which Catullus devotes entirely to bewailing his outcast state, but most notably does his tender sadness show itself in those poems in which he laments his dead brother. I remember how, when I was still a school-boy, and while still Catullus to me was perhaps not even a name, I came one day upon certain lines of that poet in Montaigne's essay on *Friendship*:

> . . O misero frater adempte mihi
> Omnia tecum una perierunt gaudia nostra. . . .
> Alloquar? audiero nunquam tua verba loquentem?
> Nunquam ego te, vita frater amabilior,
> Adspiciam posthac? at certe semper amabo;

these lines moved me greatly then—they were the first words of Catullus I knew, and to me they still seem among his loveliest.[5] Catullus the poet of passionate love is great; I am a little inclined to the heresy that Catullus the poet of overwhelming grief is greater still.

Catullus is, thirdly, the poet of deep and enduring friendship, and of the pleasant associations of life. He sings of the great joy that is his in a friend's return; of his delight in coming once more, after long exile, to his family *lares*; of his sorrow at seeing his old companions in Bithynia destitute. To be sure, indeed, behind so much of Greek and Latin masculine friendship there lurks the sinister shadow of a horrible and unnatural vice, a taint embittering all the waters of Damascus; and Catullus's friendships, unfortunately, are not wholly free from that taint. But still, despite this lurking shadow, darkening so often across a lovely page, we find in the poems of Catullus which deal with his relations with his fellows much that is thoroughly fine and attractive.

---

3   That Catullus's immediate successors thought of him primarily as a poet of love is clear enough. So Propertius, II, 25.1-4:

> Unica nata meo pulcherrima cura dolori,
> Excludit quoniam sors mea "saepe veni,"
> Ista meis fiet notissima forma libellis,
> Calve, tua venia, pace, Catulle, tua.

and again, II, 34.87:

> Haec quoque lascivi cantarunt scripta Catulli,
> Lesbia quis ipsa notior est Helena.

Ovid speaks in a like strain, *Tristia*, II, 427:

> Sic sua lascivo cantata est saepe Catullo
> Femina, cui falsum Lesbia nomen erat;
> Nec contentus ea, multos vulgavit amores,
> In quibus ipse suum fassus adulterium est.

4   Tennyson, *Frater, Ave atque Vale*.

5   The third line of the above quotation is, of course, an emendation; see Ellis, *Liber*, p. 152, and *Commentary*, pp. 351-352.

Catullus, again, is a master of pleasant humor and subtle wit. His account of his conversation with Varus's mistress (*Carm.* x), the delicate little poem on the loves of Acme and Septimius (*Carm.* xlv), and the lines on the Latin cockney, Arrius (*Carm.* lxxxiv),—these represent Catullus at his best in a light mood; while the finely pointed epigram on the pandering Gallus (*Carm.* lxxviii) must stand among the very best things of its kind in Latin poetry. But in candor it must be admitted, I think, that Catullus is not at his best as a wit,[6] and that, as an epigrammatist, he is far surpassed by his admirer Martial. He has not Martial's ability to flick sharply with the whip of his scorn; he has not Martial's dexterity and quickness of thrust, as we see these qualities, let us say, in the sparkling

> Esse tibi tanta cautus brevitate videris?
>   Ei mihi, quam multis sic quoque longus eris!

or in that vicious gem on an uncongenial helpmate:

> Omnes quae habuit, Fabiane, Lycoris amicas
>   Extulit. Uxori fiat amica meae![7]

But this, after all, is only to say that Catullus is not so clever as Martial; Milton, for that matter, is far from being so clever as Tom Hood.

Catullus is, however, the poet of fierce hate and, in the expression of that hate, of gross obscenity. To be sure, he hated, in the main, what was deserving of detestation; he inveighs against falseness in one loved, infidelity in friends, incompetence and evil doing in high places, even, indeed, gross infractions of the moral code, incest, and those lower variations of vice to which he was not himself addicted. And here, in the making of foul and savage satiric verse, it must be owned that Catullus stands on a certain eminence, though that eminence be a bad one: in certain of his *Carmina* he is at once supremely ferocious and supremely foul. But this is an aspect of Catullus's genius on which I should not willingly linger.

Another element in Catullus's character may deserve a moment's notice, his *pietas*, his desire not to sin against the divine will, his reverence for the gods, his evident desire to lead a good life as he conceived a good life, and his pathetic confidence that he had not departed from the life of rectitude. There is to me something exquisitely moving in those lovely lines in which he expresses his belief that he has not, as the Stoics would say, sinned against the law of his own nature:

> Si qua recordanti benefacta priora voluptas
>   Est homini, cum se cogitat esse pium,
> Nec sanctam violasse fidem, nec foedere in ullo
>   Divum ad fallendos numine abusum homines,
> Multa parata manent in longa aetate, Catulle. . .[8]

These qualities, then, I take to be the distinguishing marks of Catullus's poetry, fiery passion, tender sadness, a nice sensitiveness to the pleasanter aspects of human relations, delicate humor, and, sometimes, sparkling wit, the expression of fierce and often righteous hate, in which coarseness and obscenity are the weapon most employed, and, finally, a sense of reverence and respect for the divine powers. We

---

6 Quintilian, to be sure, remarks upon the *acerbitas* of his iambics (satiric epigrams), X, 1, 96, and speaks with just praise of the verses on Arrius, *Carm.* lxxxiv, as that *Catulli nobile epigramma*, I, 5, 20.

7 Martial, *Epigrammata*, II, 1, and IV, 24.

8 *Carm.* lxxvi, 1-5.

may briefly consider the divisions of Catullus's poetry, making use of these major qualities of the poet in grouping his poems.

THE DIVISIONS OF CATULLUS'S POETRY

It is difficult, indeed impossible, to divide the poems of Catullus into clearly defined groups, and say, for example, "These are all love poems and nought else; these are all poems of sorrow and of sorrow only." Catullus mingles his *genres* very frequently; a savage attack upon a company of tavern-frequenters ends with a tender reference to his mistress, and he breaks away from the narration of the loves of Laodamia and Protesilaus to mourn his brother dead in the fatal Troad. My division, then, is merely approximate, and deals, in the main, only with the major thoughts of the poems in question.

The poems of love, though far and away the most important part of Catullus's work, are comparatively few in number. Those dealing primarily with love for a mistress are:

Number   ii   Passer, deliciae meae puellae. . .

          iii   Lugete, o Veneres Cupidinesque. . .

          v   Vivamus, mea Lesbia, atque amemus. . .

          vii   Quaeris quot mihi basiationes. . .

          viii   Miser Catulle, desinas ineptire. . .

          xi   Furi et Aureli, comites Catulli. . .

       xxxii   Amabo, mea dulcis Ipsithilla. . .

     xxxvi   Annales Volusi, cacata charta. . .

        xlv   Acmen Septimius suos amores. . .

          li   Ille mi par esse deo videtur. . .

       lviii   Caeli, Lesbia nostra, Lesbia illa. . .

  lxviii-b   Non possum reticere, deae, qua me Allius in re. . .

        lxx   Nulli se dicit mulier mea nubere malle. . .

       lxxii   Dicebas quondam solum te nosse Catullum. . .

       lxxv   Huc est mens deducta tua, mea Lesbia, culpa. . .

      lxxvi   Si qua recordanti benefacta priora voluptas. . .

     lxxxii   Quinti, si tibi vis oculos debere Catullum. . .

   lxxxiii   Lesbia mi praesente viro mala plurima dicit. . .

     lxxxv   Odi et amo. Quare id faciam fortasse requiris. . .

   lxxxvi   Quintia formosa est multis, mihi candida, longa. . .

  lxxxvii   Nulla potest mulier tantum se dicere amatam. . .

        xcii   Lesbia mi dicit semper male nec tacet unquam. . .

        civ   Credis me potuisse meae maledicere vitae. . .

       cvii   Si cui quid cupido optantique obtigit unquam. . .

       cix   Iucundum, mea vita, mihi proponis amorem. . .

The poems dealing with paederastic love in the strain of a lover are five in number:

Number   xv   Commendo tibi me ac meos amores. . .

       xxiv   O qui flosculus es Iuventiorum. . .

     xlviii   Mellitos oculos tuos, Iuventi. . .

      lxxxi   Nemone in tanto potuit populo esse, Iuventi. . .

       xcix   Subripui tibi, dum ludis, mellite Iuventi. . .

The poems dealing more indirectly with love are the epithalamia:
Number lxi Collis o Heliconii. . .
          lxii Vesper adest: iuvenes, consurgite: Vesper Olympo. . .
and the narrative poems:
Number lxiii Super alta vectus Attis celeri rate maria. . .
          lxiv Peliaco quondam prognatae vertice pinus. . .
          lxvi Omnia qui magni dispexit lumina mundi. . .

The poems in which the element of sadness predominates are:
Number xxx Alfene immemor atque unanimis false sodalibus. . .
      xxxviii Male est, Cornifici, tuo Catullo. . .
            lx Num te leaena montibus Libystinis. . .
          lxv Etsi me adsiduo defectum cura dolore. . .
    lxviii-a Quod mihi fortuna casuque oppressus acerbo. . .
        lxxiii Desine de quoquam quicquam bene velle mereri. . .
          xcvi Si quicquam mutis gratum acceptumve sepulcris. . .
            ci Multas per gentes et multa per aequora vectus. . .

The poems in which love for friends and interest in home and in the pleasant
intercourse of ordinary life play the major parts are:
Number   i Cui dono lepidum novum libellum. . .
            iv Phasellus ille, quem videtis, hospites. . .
            vi Flavi, delicias tuas Catullo. . .
            ix Verani, omnibus e meis amicis. . .
            x Varus me meus ad suos amores. . .
          xiv Ni te plus oculis meis amarem. . .
        xxvi Furi, villula vestra non ad Austri. . .
      xxvii Minister vetuli puer Falerni. . .
    xxviii Pisonis comites, cohors inanis. . .
        xxxi Paene insularum, Sirmio, insularumque. . .
      xxxv Poetae tenero, meo sodali. . .
        xlvi Iam ver egelidos refert tepores. . .
        xlvii Porci et Socration, duae sinistrae. . .
        xlix Disertissime Romuli nepotum. . .
            l Hesterno, Licini, die otiosi. . .
          liii Risi nescio quem modo e corona. . .
      lxxvii Rufe mihi frustra ac nequiquam credite amice. . .
          xcv Zmyrna mei Cinnae nonam post denique messem. . .
            c Caelius Aufilenum et Quintius Aufilenam. . .
          cii Si quicquam tacito commissum est fido ab amico. . .

The jesting poems and the less ferocious epigrams include a number of those
already listed as being addressed to his friends, and in addition include:
Number xiii Cenabis bene, mi Fabulle, apud me. . .
        xliv O funde noster seu Sabine seu Tiburs. . .
          lv Oramus, si forte non molestum est. . .
      lxxviii Gallus habet fratres, quorum est lepidissima coniunx. . .
      lxxxiv Chommoda dicebat, si quando commoda vellet. . .

The savagely satiric poems, and those in which invective or vulgar humor are most important, form a class rather larger than any other.[9] These are, in my enumeration:

Number   xii   Marrucine Asini, manu sinistra. . .
          xvi   Pedicabo ego vos et irrumabo. . .
         xvii   O Colonia, quae cupis ponte ludere longo . . .
          xxi   Aureli, pater esuritionum. . .
         xxii   Suffenus iste, Vare, quem probe nosti. . .
        xxiii   Furi, cui neque servus est neque arca. . .
         xxv   Cinaede Thalle, mollior cuniculi capillo. . .
        xxix   Quis hoc potest videre, quis potest pati. . .
      xxxiii   O furum optime balneariorum. . .
     xxxvii   Salax taberna vosque contubernales. . . .
     xxxix   Egnatius, quod candidos habet dentes. . .
           xl   Quaenam te mala mens, miselle Ravide. . .
          xli   Ameana, puella defututa. . .
        xlii   Adeste, hendecasyllabi, quot estis. . .
       xliii   Salve, nec minimo puella naso. . .
          lii   Quid est, Catulle? quid moraris emori? . . .
         liv   Othonis caput oppido est pusillum. . .
         lvi   O rem ridiculam, Cato, et iocosam. . .
        lvii   Pulchre convenit improbis cinaedis. . .
         lix   Bononiensis Rufa Rufulum fellat. . .
      lxvii   O dulci iucunda viro, iucunda parenti. . .
       lxix   Noli admirari quare tibi femina nulla. . .
       lxxi   Si cui iure bono sacer alarum obstitit hircus. . .
      lxxiv   Gellius audierat patruum obiurgare solere. . .
  lxxviii-b   Sed nunc id doleo quod purae pura puellae. . .
      lxxix   Lesbius est pulcher: quid ni? quem Lesbia malit. . .
      lxxx   Quid dicam, Gelli, quare rosea ista labella. . .
   lxxxviii   Quid facit is, Gelli, qui cum matre atque sorore. . .
   lxxxix   Gellius est tenius: quid ni? cui tam bona mater. . .
          xc   Nascatur magus ex Gelli matrisque nefando. . .
          xci   Non ideo, Gelli, sperabam te mihi fidum. . .
        xciii   Nil nimium studeo, Caesar, tibi velle placere. . .
        xciv   Mentula moechatur. Moechatur mentula certe. . .
      xcvii   Non (ita me di ament) quicquam referre putavi. . .
     xcviii   In te, si in quemquam, dici pote, putide Victi. . .
        ciii   Aut sodes mihi redde decem sestertia, Silo. . .
          cv   Mentula conatur Pipleum scandere montem. . .
         cvi   Cum puero bello praeconem qui videt esse. . .
       cviii   Si, Comini, populi arbitrio tua cana senectus. . .
          cx   Aufilena, bonae semper laudantur amicae. . .

9 K. P. Harrington, *Catullus and his Influence*, pp. 52-53: "There are really only twenty-odd, mostly short, poems which deal directly with the love of Catullus. . . . There are twice as many poems of hatred, sometimes extended about to the traditional 'forty stripes.' "

> cxi   Aufilena, viro contentam vivere solo. . .
> cxii   Multus homo est, Naso, neque tecum multus homo est qui. . .
> cxiii Consule Pompeio primum duo, Cinna, solebant. . .
> cxiv   Firmanus saltu non falso Mentula dives. . .
> cxv   Mentula habet iuxta triginta iugera prati. . .
> cxvi   Saepe tibi studioso animo venante requiris. . .

There is one purely religious poem among the *Carmina*, xxxiv, addressed to Diana:

> Dianae sumus in fide
> Puellae et pueri integri. . .

The Priapian poems, numbers xviii, xix, and xx in certain of the editions of Catullus, are definitely not his,[10] and, even in the seventeenth century, the period of our study, they were not regarded as belonging to Catullus.[11] I have disregarded them throughout, as unworthy of being fathered upon Catullus. For the purposes of this study I have felt justified in being somewhat arbitrary in rejecting them; it is primarily a matter for the classical scholar, but the weight of authority is overwhelmingly on my side.

CATULLUS IN SEVENTEENTH CENTURY ENGLAND

Such, then, are, in my estimation, the chief characteristics of Catullus, and such are, roughly, the divisions of his poetry. It remains to discover how these qualities were appreciated by the lyric poets of the early seventeenth century, and what use they made of the various kinds of poetry written by Catullus.

One should make clear at once, however, that the influence of Catullus in English poetry was a manifestation of comparatively late appearance and of slow growth. "It is clear," says Professor Harrington, "that Catullus was not one of the first Latin poets to become popular in England. . . Virgil, Horace, and Ovid were widely known in Europe when Catullus was in obscurity, and they became popular in England before he was generally known to the English public."[12] He quotes from Miss Palmer's treatise on *English Editions and Translations of Greek and Latin Classics Printed before 1641*,[13] pointing out that there appears but a single entry under "Catullus"—"an edition of the *Phasellus ille* poem with such parodies on it as were then extant"; on the other hand, "the same list contains the titles of thirty-five editions or translations of the whole or part of the works of Horace." Professor Harrington then goes on to quote Professor Berdan's explanation of the early supremacy of Horace over Catullus in English poetry, whereas Catullus was the favorite poet of Italy. The explanation Mr. Berdan finds in the different temper of the peoples. "The fire and passion of Catullus found a congenial soil in Italy;" but the "cold, restrained, northern nature felt more at ease with the philosophy of Horace,"

---

10   Among modern editors, Ellis, Postgate, Owen, Merrill and Baehrens reject the Priapian poems.

11   In an edition of Catullus which I have now before me, edited by Gabbema, and published in 1659, the Priapian poems are printed, indeed, but printed in a type different from that of the others, to indicate their being spurious.

12   Harrington, *op. cit.*, pp. 139-140.

13   p. 26.

for "in Tudor England, humanism was a serious, moral, reflective force."[14] The reasons, then, for the comparatively slight influence of Catullus upon early English poetry are, in the estimation of Professor Harrington and Professor Berdan, first, his coming late into competition with such poets as Horace, Vergil, and Ovid, when they had already secured a virtual supremacy, and, secondly, the essential difference in temper between the passionate verses of Catullus and the more reflective mood of Tudor poetry.

In the period of our study, however, those years focusing in that great half century of English lyric expression, 1600 to 1650, we find that Catullus has come into his own as a great motivating, moulding force in English poetry. Even then, to be sure, he did not have the universality of appeal that Horace has so long possessed; Catullus remained, in the main, the poet's poet, and not the scholar's. Learned divines and erudite savants found in him no weighty apophthegms, no ponderous platitudes, no long-rolling and loud-resounding declamations, no pithy comments on literature, and no such quotable stylistic rules as the profound warning against the monstrosity that would result should

> . . .Turpiter atrum
> Desinat in piscem mulier formosa superne.

Furthermore, the scholarship of the day looked askance upon the period which had in Catullus its greatest poetical representative. "Of the inimitable beauties of the Latin poets of the prae-Augustan age," says Mullinger, "there is not a glimpse of anything like adequate recognition: the rhetorical strains of Lucan, on the other hand, were. . . generally admired."[15]

The mention of Lucan brings us to another characteristic of the period which militated against wider recognition of Catullus, namely, that perverted erudition which led men of learning into the byways and sometimes, indeed, morasses of Latin scholarship, to the neglect of the fair, broad ways.

> The researches of young classical students [says Mullinger again] appear to have extended to authors which a private tutor of the present day would probably look somewhat coldly upon, when viewed in connection with the Tripos. 'I afterwards finished Florus,' writes D'Ewes, 'transcribing historical abbreviations out of it in my own private study; in which also I perused most of the other authors and read over Gellius' *Attic Nights*, and part of Macrobius' *Saturnals*.[16]

But, if misdirected erudition be responsible in part for a lack of knowledge of Catullus in various quarters, just the opposite reason, ignorance, would account for the absence of any knowledge of the great Latin poet in such young gallants as Suckling or Aurelian Townshend. Margaret Duchess of Newcastle's description of the education of her husband (himself, in his later days, an assiduous versifier) is indicative, I take it, of the early classical education of many a courtly poet and poetaster:

> His education was according to his birth; for as he was born a gentleman, so he was bred like a gentleman. To school-learning he never showed a great inclination; for though he was sent to the university, and was a student at St. John's Col-

---

14   J. M. Berdan, *Early Tudor Poetry*, pp. 261-262.
15   J. B. Mullinger, *Cambridge Characteristics in the Seventeenth Century*, p. 56.
16   *Op. cit.*, p. 54.

lege in Cambridge, and had his tutors to instruct him; yet they could not persuade him to read or study much, he taking more delight in sports than in learning.[17]

But if the learned pedants and divines and the courtly rhymers of the day made no great use of Catullus, the real poets of that great lyric age recognized in him a model for lyrical form, and a source of true inspiration, as the pages which follow well attest. The poets of the age, to be sure, fall roughly into three groups, those who chose as their tutelary poetic saint either Spenser, or Ben Jonson, or Donne. In the followers of Jonson, and, to a less degree, in the followers of Spenser, the classical element is large; in many of the imitators of Donne it may assume very small porportions indeed. Now in the proportion that the poetry of the age is most *metaphysical*, in the manner of Donne, in that proportion is it sure of being far from any classical inspiration, and, in particular, from the manner of that least "metaphysical" of poets, Catullus. In two of the great schools of poetry of the age we may look to find notable evidences of Catullian influence; in the third, we shall find that, by and large, intellectual niceties have swallowed up both the classical and the poetic.

But we may well turn now to a consideration of the use which the poets of the seventeenth century made of the various types of Catullus's poetry, and to a comparison, short and elementary, necessarily, of the temper of that age with that which has its greatest poetical prototype in Catullus.

It will be seen from the pages that follow that it was by his love poetry that Catullus exerted the greatest influence on the English poets of the seventeenth century. Certain of the poems addressed to Lesbia, in particular ii, iii, vii, and lxx, and, far and away the most often translated and paraphrased of all, the famous *Vivamus, mea Lesbia, atque amemus*—these are the poems which reappear, in one form or another, in most of the notable poets of the period of this study.[18] The Epithalamia of Catullus are perhaps next in point of frequency of occurrence and depth of influence—there arose what one might call a "Catullian formula" in the making of epithalamia,[19] a formula which became so much a part of English poetic tradition that we may see a poet, apparently otherwise oblivious of Catullus, making an epithalamium on the model of the famous sixty-first *carmen*, that on the nuptials of Vinia and Manlius.

The poets of our period, I have said, modeled themselves upon Catullus in their love poetry, but in those two distinguishing qualities of Catullus's poetry, his simplicity and his passion, the *"simplicité passionnée"* of Fénelon, they fell, very often, far short of the Roman lyrist.

Again and again, in reading the English love poetry of this period, we feel that the poet is playing with the passion; he is singing because he can, or because it is the thing to do, not because he must. This is not to say, for it would be gross absurdity

17   *The Life of the First Duke of Newcastle*, Book 3, Section 8.
18   It may be helpful to note the translations of *Carm.* v. (and, in general, the references to it) as they appear in this study: CAMPION, (1) (2); RALEIGH, (1); DANIEL, (1); DONNE (2); SONG BOOKS, (4) (6); JONSON, (1) (2); RANDOLPH, (6); CARTWRIGHT, (11); DRUMMOND (9) (12); CRASHAW, (2); HABINGTON, (5); BROME, (1); HERRICK, (5) (9) (10) (24) (33) (42); MARVELL, (1) (3); COWLEY, (4); SHERBURNE, (1).
19   For a very interesting discussion of this type of poetry and of the classical influence upon it, see the Introduction to R. H. Case's *English Epithalamies*.

to do so, that there is not much that is sincere and heart-felt and deeply moving in Jacobean and Caroline love poetry; what I do say is that, compared with the over-mastering passion of Catullus, much of the poetry of this period rings hollow. Lafaye has well said that

> La passion de Catulle pour Lesbie a rempli sa pensée pendant plusieurs années; elle est la plus grand événement de sa vie; elle domine toute son oeuvre lyrique.[20]

There is no English poet of the period of our study of whom the like could be said. They fondle their love, and ring changes upon their passion, but it is very rarely that they feel it deeply. So we have poem after poem "against fruition":

> Hopes joined with doubts, and joys with April tears,
> That crowns our love with pleasures; these are gone
> When once we come to full fruition. . . .
> O what a stroke 'twould be! sure I should die,
> Should I but hear my mistress once say, ay.[21]

This is not the language of love, but of a watery and affected gallantry, utterly foreign to Catullus. Then there is the ever recurring insistence upon the transitori-ness of love and upon the fragility of lovers' protestations, not, as we find like sen-timents in Catullus, written in regret or sorrow, but in a tone of utter cynicism:

> Why should'st thou swear I am forsworn,
>   Since thine I vow'd to be?
> Lady, it is already morn,
>   And 'twas last night I swore to thee
>   That fond impossibility.[22]

Attendant upon this lack of sincerity comes, naturally, a like lack of simplicity; ingenuity is called in to take the place of deep feeling. The intellect speaks when the heart is silent, and embroiders on themes which are often taken, not from personal experience, but from the recorded emotions of others. Drummond, who would have every claim to be considered a great poet if great poetry consisted in rhyming exquisitely the thoughts of others, has inadvertently phrased, in a few lines put into the mouth of a disdainful lady, a lasting criticism of much of his own love poetry and of the love poetry of others of his period:

> Strephon, in vain thou bring'st thy rhymes and songs. . .
> Thou hast slept never under myrtles' shed,
> Or, if that passion hath thy soul oppress'd,
> It is but for some Grecian mistress dead. . .
> I cannot think thou wert charm'd by my looks,
> O no, thou learn'dst thy love in lovers' books.[23]

But the rhyming of a "Grecian mistress dead," however much it may have taken from the sincerity of the poetry so composed, was productive of very real simplicity of form and clearness of expression; it was when the mind of the poet, turned inward upon itself, produced, as it so often did, fine-drawn original conceits and wearyingly ingenious analogies or similes, it was then, I repeat, that English poetry departed utterly from the spirit of Catullus.

20   Lafaye, *Les Poésies de Catulle*, p. x.
21   Sir John Suckling, *Against Fruition* (Thompson, p. 29).
22   Lovelace, *The Scrutinie* (Caxton Club edition, I, p. 105).
23   Drummond, *Five Sonnets for Galatea*, I (*Muses Library Edition*, II, p. 127).

But we might protract this discussion interminably, bringing forward example after example in support of our point that, although English love poetry of the seventeenth century drew heavily upon Catullus, it was indebted rather to the body and substance of his work than to its spirit, for to the passionate earnestness and simple vehemence of the Latin poet it very seldom approached.

But English poetry, if less simple and passionate than the love poetry of Catullus, was far more sensuous, and sensuous in the derogatory sense of the word. The poems of Catullus which are addressed to the woman he really loved are written, in the main, in the language of the most profound respect, and even when, in his despair and sorrow, he speaks of Lesbia in anger, he still retains a certain sad dignity:

> Credis me potuisse meae maledicere vitae,
>   Ambobus mihi quae carior est oculis?
> Non potui, nec, si possem, tam perdite amarem.[24]

It is only the women whom he cares little about, Ameana or Ipsithilla, that he condescends to address in the language of loose gallantry. The esteem in which Catullus held the woman he dearly loved was far different from that of the rake Cartwright:

> Give me a girl (if one I needs must meet)
> Or in her nuptial, or her winding sheet;
> I know but two good hours that women have,
> One in the bed, another in the grave.
> Thus of the whole sex all I would desire,
> Is to enjoy their ashes, or their fire.[25]

This is not to say, of course, that the age in which Catullus lived and, indeed, Catullus himself, were not more corrupt than the seventeenth century, for more corrupt he and his age surely were;[26] it is to say, however, that where Catullus deeply loved he respected deeply, and that the English poets, who very often were but playing with a fictitious flame, felt themselves free to embroider upon that passion with all the luxuriance of a lascivious fancy. One need but turn to Herrick's poem to Anthea (see HERRICK, 5) for an illustration. Here Herrick has chosen the famous fifth *carmen* of Catullus, but, whereas Catullus in addressing his lady has kept his verses utterly clear of any close reference to the physical, Herrick concludes his little poem in a vein utterly gross and earthy. I shall not elaborate this difference between the love poetry of Catullus and much of the love poetry of the seventeenth century, yet the subject, I think, merits consideration at some little length. Much, to be sure, is summed up in Byron's illuminating words:

> A true voluptary [and we may substitute, I think, "a true poet of love"] will never abandon his mind to the grossness of reality. It is by excluding the earthly, the material, the *physical* of our pleasures, by veiling these ideas, or, at least, never naming them hardly to oneself, that we alone can prevent them from disgusting.[27]

---

24 *Carm.* civ.
25 Cartwright, *Women* (Goffin, p. 39).
26 Dunlop (*History of Latin Literature to the Augustan Age*, I, pp. 498-499) says with justice of *Carm.* lxi: "The coarse imitation of the Fescennine poems leaves on our minds a stronger impression of the prevalence and extent of Roman vices than any other passage in the Latin classics... Here in a complimentary poem to a patron and intimate friend these [sodomitic practices of the bridegroom] are jocularly alluded to as the venial indulgence of his earliest youth."
27 Quoted in Professor H. J. C. Grierson's *The Background of English Literature*, p. 79.

The paederastic love poems of Catullus were comparatively little used by the poets of this study; Lovelace translates one or two of them, and one finds occasional phrases borrowed from them occurring now and then in a few poets. They are good love poems enough, *mutatis mutandis*, but the paederastic taint was too strong for the English poets to look with favor upon them.

Catullus's poems of sorrow were made far less use of than one might expect. Ariadne's complaint, in *Carm.* lxiv, is, indeed, very frequently drawn upon, but the *Attis* (*Carm.* lxiii) seems almost unheeded. That great poem in which Catullus pays his last tribute to the shade of his departed brother (*Carm.* ci) is rarely met with, highly esteemed though it is today. Indeed, Catullus's expressions of grief play a surprisingly small part in influencing the elegies and consolatory poems of our period. Professor Grierson says, with great justice:

> In general, seventeenth century elegy is apt to spend itself on three not easily reconcilable themes—extravagant eulogy of the dead, which is the characteristically Renaissance strain, the Medieval meditation on death and its horrors, the more simply Christian mood of hope rising at times to the rapt vision of a higher life.[28]

Into no one of these methods of mourning did Catullus's poignant expression of personal grief over the eternal loss of a dear one easily fit, with the result that his influence upon elegiacal verse is comparatively slight.

The lighter poems of Catullus, dealing with his daily life and with his relations towards his friends, were not greatly drawn upon by the poets of our period. The Sirmio poem (*Carm.* xxxi) and Catullus's poem on his pinnace (*Carm.* iv), so often translated and so much admired today, seem to have appealed very little to the poets of the seventeenth century. The invitation to Fabullus (*Carm.* xiii) is very popular, but the exceedingly amusing account of Catullus's conversation with Varus's mistress is utterly neglected. Many of the satiric epigrams of Catullus reappear in one form or another, but it is their form rather than their substance that is most influential. In adapting Catullus's epigrams the Jacobean or Caroline poet did not, in most instances, feel called upon to make use of Catullus's filth, but made use of his own equally nauseous store.[29] Catullus's one religious poem, the Hymn to Diana, *Carm.* xxxiv, found, naturally enough, no echo in English verse.

This must suffice for a brief summary of the influence of Catullus; the succeeding pages offer many examples and amplifications of what I have here said. They show, far more clearly than any comment in this place, how embracing his influence was and what directions that influence took.

THE LATER INFLUENCE OF CATULLUS

The influence of Catullus did not, of course, come to anything like a close at the end of the period I have here dealt with, as Professor Harrington and Professor Duckett have helped to make clear.[30] To their labors, in my own period, I have been greatly indebted, not so much for matter as for guidance in the direction of my work. I think I may justly say that, within its more limited range, this treatise is

28   Grierson, *Donne's Poetical Works*, II, p. xxvi.
29   For a case in point, see my chapter on Sir John Davies, pp. 34-35.
30   K. P. Harrington, *Catullus and His Influence.*
     Eleanor Shipley Duckett, *Catullus in English Poetry.*

somewhat more thorough than those of the scholars I have just mentioned; so, where Professor Harrington has instanced, according to my reckoning, some sixteen cases of Catullian influence upon Herrick, I have instanced forty-two. The period of this study is, indeed, that in which the influence of Catullus in English poetry was most pronounced, in part because it is the age that marks a turning aside from subservience to the contemporary poetry of the continent, and, in Moorman's phrase, "a return to the greater directness and less etherial temper of the classical lyric of Anacreon, Catullus, and Horace."[31] Finally, when I draw my study to a close, the true lyric spirit of the early half of the century has waned, yielding to the frigid graces of Waller and the empty clevernesses of Prior. With the coming of the Augustan age Catullus's influence falls for a time into abeyance, though there are poets, Swift, for example, and Prior himself, who show a certain knowledge and appreciation of his peculiar merits. But Catullus holds no longer the place he once had, and Addison's amazing judgment represents fairly enough, I suppose, the temper of the age. For Addison, in an essay upon the Roman poets in which he can find it in his heart to praise the poetry of Seneca and Claudian, concludes with a sentence which may well take its place as a signal example of a great man blundering egregiously:

> Caeterum tamen Poetarum Vulgus, de istiusmodi mediocribus sunt, quos nec Dii nec Homines concesserunt; et quamvis una aut altera *apud affectatas Catulli Oratiunculas*, Tibulli aut Propertii inhonestam paginam, et Carmina incuriosa, illucescat Virtus, non tamen est Operae Pretium Gemmas inter Stercora eruere.[32]

THE DETAILS OF SELECTION AND QUOTATION

In choosing the following passages I have preferred, in deciding between two evils, to err on the side of completeness rather than on the side of incompleteness. That is, when I was in doubt whether any passage showed a clear trace of the influence of Catullus or not, I have usually decided to retain it. I recognize that many references, frequently occurring in these pages, to "the ivy and the elm," for example, and to "saffron Hymen", cannot always be traced, with entire justice, to Catullus; I have not included such passing references, as a rule, unless the context seemed to offer at least a reasonable basis for assuming a borrowing from Catullus. For, though one can not *always* be sure that a reference to "the vine and the elm" is definitely inspired by Catullus, one can *never* be sure that it is not.

THE TEXT

I have made greatest use, in so far as the Latin text is concerned, of the great edition of Robinson Ellis[33] and of the excellent American edition of E. T. Merrill. The latter, indeed, I have made most use of in my quotations, as Merrill's text, which is normalized in spelling throughout, I found better suited to my purposes than the more exact (so far as the manuscripts are concerned) but, necessarily, more erratic text of Ellis. In short, I have sought to have in this study a Latin text convenient and easily readable, rather than a Latin text minutely, but, for my pur-

---

31 Moorman, *Cambridge History of English Literature*, VIII, p. 2.
32 Addison, *Dissertatio de Insignioribus Romanorum Poetis* (Guthkelch, II, p. 476-477).
33 Robinson Ellis, *Catulli Veronensis Liber*, Oxonii, 1867.

poses, unnecessarily exact. I have also made much use of several other editions of Catullus, notably Lafaye's and Owen's excellent editions.

The text of the English poems I have, in most instances, normalized, feeling that in a work of this kind nothing, or very little, would be gained by retaining spellings at best unhelpful and at worst perplexing.

THE DEFINITION OF LYRIC POETRY

I have used a very liberal definition of "lyric" in this paper, not merely using the term to cover short poems with a poignantly personal element, but, indeed, as a general term to cover all poems which are not distinctly narrative or dramatic, but, in the broadest sense, personal. I have, moreover, for the sake of completeness, included much that is in no sense lyrical, quotations, for example, from Jonson's plays. But by far the greater part of the pages which follow are concerned only with poetry of lyric quality.

THOMAS CAMPION
(c. 1567-1620)

Of the poets considered in this paper, no other, with the single exception of Herrick, is so truly Catullian, in manner and inspiration, as Thomas Campion. He is, in a very true sense, the most lyrical of them all; "his lyre was a real instrument; that is to say, it was represented by real instruments, the lute and the viol;"[1] —his poems were written primarily to be sung, only secondarily to be read. They have those prime requisites of good lyrical poetry, lucidity and simplicity, and they place him, without peer, in the very front rank of the song-writers of his age. "It is largely on Campion's verses that the general high opinion of Elizabethan song is founded";[2] "when all has been said, in Thomas Campion we reach the prince of this tuneful realm of Elizabethan song";[3] Thomas Campion is "the one poet who comes nearest to fulfilling in his work the lyric canon in English poetry"[4]—these are the constantly recurring phrases of the critics in speaking of Campion. Now, just in the proportion that Campion is a true lyric poet, just in the proportion that he is "simple, sensuous, and passionate," just in the proportion that a critic may justly speak of "the freshness and spontaneous charm of Campion's lyrics, concealing, as they do, beneath their seemingly artless ease, a subtle mastery of syllabic tones and values,"[5] in that proportion is he akin, in manner and method, to the master lyrist Catullus.

But this resemblance, this fellowship, is not merely a likeness of chance; it came in large part from loving knowledge and imitation. For Campion was a thorough classicist; indeed, in theory, at least, too thorough a classicist, for, had he followed the principle which he preached in his *Observations on the Art of English Poesy*, excessive and slavish devotion to the classics would have meant for him, as it did for Harvey and many another man, ruin and oblivion. But, as an Irish critic well points out, the poet within him saved him from the scholar, and barely saved him. "He was a scholar in an age of much wrong-headed learning. He was a sweet singer in an age of song. He wrote more poems in Latin than in English. He wrote of English verse as if it were imitation Latin verse. He tried to train himself in a foreign mode of poetic speech."[6] As it happened, he escaped the evil consequences of his knowledge, and reaped, in the main, only its advantages; his acquaintance with the classics gave him, instead of dullness and obscurity, ease, grace, inimitable delicacy, and lucidity. "The inspiration of Campion," says Schelling, "is more directly classical than that of almost any lyrist of his immediate time. Campion's limpidity of diction, his choice placing and selection of words, his perfect taste and melody, and his devotion to love, all are qualities which disclose how steeped he was in the poetry of Tibullus and Catullus."[7]

1 Ernest Rhys, *Lyric Poetry*, p. 171.
2 John Erskine, *The Elizabethan Lyric*, p. 231.
3 Schelling, *English Literature during the Lifetime of Shakespeare*, p. 199.
4 Rhys, *loc. cit.*, p. 171.
5 S. Percival Vivian, in *Cambridge History of English Literature*, IV, p. 171.
6 Thomas MacDonagh, *Thomas Campion and the Art of English Poetry*, p. 4.
7 Schelling, *English Literature during the Lifetime of Shakespeare*, pp. 199-200.

To Catullus, of all the Latin poets, he was perhaps most closely akin; he refers to Catullus, specifically, now and again, in a way which indicates that he considered him the typical lyric poet among the ancients; so, in his "Address to the Reader," preceding the *First Book of Airs*, he says, "Airs have both their art and pleasure; and I will conclude of them, as the poet did in censure of Catullus the Lyric, and Virgil the Heroic writer:

> Tantum magna suo debet Verona Catullo
> Quantum parva suo Mantua Virgilio;"[8]

again it is Catullus (this time, with Martial) that he calls to his aid in another argumentative address "To the Reader": "Others taste nothing that comes forth in print; as if Catullus' or Martial's *Epigrams* were the worse for being published."[9] My acquaintance with his Latin works is very limited; they show, says Vivian, "a considerable familiarity with the Latin poets,"[10] and are in large part imitative. For example, one of the epigrams, *Ad Ed. Spencerum*:[11]

> Sive canis silvas, Spencere, vel horrida belli
> Fulmina, dispeream ni te amem, et intime amem,

has a very clear echo of Catullus's (*Carm.* xcii):

> Deprecor illam
> Adsidue, verum dispeream nisi amo.

Miss Duckett quotes another of his epigrams, referring specifically to Catullus and to one of the most epigrammatic of Catullus's poems:

> Cum tibi vilescat doctus lepidusque Catullus;
>   Non est ut sperem, Cambre, placere tibi.
> Tu quoque cum Suffenorum suffragia quaeras;
>   Non est ut speres, Cambre, placere mihi.[12]

Here the reference is, of course, to *Carm.* xxii. I should hazard the assertion that a careful student would find many more instances of the influence of Catullus upon the Latin verses of Campion.

Be that as it may, the influence of the Latin poet upon Campion is very considerable and sufficiently evident, as the following passages testify. Here, as elsewhere, I have included lyrical passages drawn from the dramatic works of the author under consideration; Campion's masques, as Vivian points out, contain some of his best songs, and are full of "lyrical moments."[13]

(1)   From *A Book of Airs*, I (Bullen, p. 7):

> My sweetest Lesbia, let us live and love;
> And though the sager sort our deeds reprove,
> Let us not weigh them: heaven's great lamps do dive
> Into their west, and straight again revive:
> But soon as once is set our little light,
> Then must we sleep one ever-during night. . . .

---

8   Bullen, *Works of Thomas Campion*, p. 5.
9   *Op. cit.*, p. 45.
10   Vivian, *op. cit.*, p. 160.
11   Quoted by Vivian in his introduction to the *Poetical Works of Thomas Campion*, Muses Library, p. xlv.
12   Eleanor S. Duckett, *Catullus in English Poetry*, p. 73.
13   Vivian, *Cambridge History of English Literature*, IV, p. 178.

But fools do live, and waste their little light,
And seek with pain their ever-during night. . . .

And, Lesbia, close up thou my little light,
And crown with love my ever-during night.

See *Carm.* v. 1-6:

Vivamus, mea Lesbia, atque amemus,
Rumoresque senum severiorum
Omnes unius aestimemus assis.
Soles occidere et redire possunt:
Nobis cum semel occidit brevis lux
Nox est perpetua una dormienda.

(2) *Ibid.*, IV (Bullen, p. 10):
Follow thy fair sun, unhappy shadow. . . .
Follow her! while yet her glory shineth;
There comes a luckless night,
That will dim all her light.

Almost certainly an echo of *Carm.* v., 4-6, above.

(3) *Ibid.*, V (Bullen, pp. 10-11):
My love hath vowed he will forsake me,
    And I am already sped;
Far other promise did he make me
    When he had my maidenhead. . . .

Dissembling wretch, to gain thy pleasure,
    What didst thou not vow and swear?
So didst thou rob me of my treasure
    Which so long I held so dear.
Now thou provest to me a stranger;
    Such is the vile disguise of men
When a woman is in danger.

That heart is nearest to misfortune
    That will trust a feigned tongue;
When flattering men our loves importune
    They intend us deepest wrong.

Quite probably inspired by Ariadne's complaint, *Carm.* lxiv. 139-148:

At non haec quondam blanda promissa dedisti
Voce mihi, non haec miserae sperare iubebas,
Sed connubia laeta, sed optatos hymenaeos:
Quae cuncta aerei discerpunt irrita venti.
Nunc iam nulla viro iuranti femina credat,
Nulla viri speret sermones esse fideles

Quis dum aliquid cupiens animus praegestit apisci,
Nil metuunt iurare, nihil promittere parcunt:
Sed simul ac cupidae mentis satiata libido est,
Dicta nihil meminere, nihil periuria curant.

(4) *Ibid.*, VII (Bullen, p. 12):
What harvest half so sweet is
As still to reap the kisses
　　Grown ripe in sowing?. . . .
Then what we sow,
　　With our lips let us reap, love's gains dividing!

See *Carm.* xlviii. 5-6:

Non si densior aridis aristis
Sit nostrae seges osculationis.

(5) *Ibid.*, X, Part 2 (Bullen, p. 32):
My object now must be the air:
To write in water words of fire.
See *Carm.* lxx. 3-4:
　　. . . Sed mulier cupido quod dicit amanti
　　　　In vento et rapida scribere oportet aqua.

(6) From *Divine and Moral Songs*, VI (Bullen, p. 52):
All earthly pomp or beauty to express,
Is but to carve in snow, *in waves to write.*
This, too, may be an echo of *Carm.* lxx. 3-4, above.

(7) From *Two Books of Airs:　Divine and Moral Songs*, XIX (Bullen, p. 60):
Lighten, heavy heart, thy sprite,
　　The joys recall that thence are fled;
Yield thy breast some living light;
　　The man that nothing doth is dead. . . .
Sloth the worst and best confounds:
　　It is the ruin of mankind.
This, to my mind, bears a considerable resemblance to *Carm.* li. 13-16:
Otium, Catulle, tibi molestum est:
Otio exsultas nimiumque gestis.
Otium et reges prius et beatas
　　Perdidit urbes.

(8) From the *Second Book of Airs*, III (Bullen, p. 67):
Harden now thy tired heart with more than flinty rage!
Ne'er let her false tears henceforth thy constant grief assuage!
Once true happy days thou sawst when she stood firm and kind,
Both as one then lived and held one ear, one tongue, one mind:
But now those bright hours be fled, and never may return;
What then remains but her untruths to mourn?

Silly traitress, who shall now thy careless tresses place?
Who thy pretty talk supply, whose ear thy music grace?
Who shall thy bright eyes admire? what lips triumph with thine?
Day by day who'll visit thee and say, "Th'art only mine"?
Such a time there was, God wot, but such shall never be:
Too oft, I fear, thou wilt remember me.

This is obviously modeled, in theme and manner, on Catullus's famous renunciation of Lesbia, *Carm.* viii:

Miser Catulle, desinas ineptire,
Fulsere quondam candidi tibi soles,
Cum ventitabas quo puella ducebat,
Amata nobis quantum amabitur nulla. . . .
Vale, puella! iam Catullus obdurat,
Nec te requiret nec rogabit invitam:
At tu dolebis, cum rogaberis nulla.
Scelesta, vae te! quae tibi manet vita!
Quis nunc te adibit? cui videberis bella?
Quem nunc amabis? cuius esse diceris?
Quem basiabis? cui labella mordebis?

(9) *Ibid.*, X (Bullen, p. 74):

The dove alone expresses
Her fervency in kisses,
    Of all most loving. . . .

This may very well be an echo of *Carm.* lxviii. 125-127:

Nec tantum ..... gavisa est ulla columbo
    Compar, quae multo dicitur improbius
Oscula mordenti semper decerpere rostro.

(10)   From the *Second Book of Airs*, XVIII (Bullen, p. 81):

Sooner may you count the stars,
    And number hail downpouring,
Tell the osiers of the Thames,
    Or Goodwin sands devouring,
Than the thick-showered kisses here
    Which now thy tired lips must bear.
Such a harvest never was,
    So rich and full of pleasure. . . .

See *Carm.* vii. 3-4, 7-8:

Quam magnus numerus [basiationum] Libyssae harenae
Laserpiciferis iacet Cyrenis. . . .
Aut quam sidera multa, cum tacet nox,
Furtivos hominum vident amores.

For the last two lines, see *Carm.* xlviii. 5-6, and (4) above.

(11)   From the *Third Book of Airs*, XXI (Bullen, p. 104):
> This I resolve, and time hath taught me so,
>   Since she is fair and ever kind to me,
> Though she be wild and wanton-like in show,
>   These little stains in youth I will not see.
> That she be constant, heaven I oft implore:
> If prayers prevail not, I can do no more.

This is distinctly reminiscent of *Carm.* lxviii. 135-137:
> Quae tamenetsi uno non est contenta Catullo,
>   Rara verecundae furta feremus erae,
> Ne nimium simus stultorum more molesti.

(12)   From the *Masque at the Marriage of Lord Hayes* (Bullen, p. 155):
> *Can.*   Who is the happier of the two,
>   A maid, or wife?
> *Ten.*   Which is the more to be desired,
>   Peace or strife?. . . .
> *Ten.*   A maid is free, a wife is tied.
> *Can.*   No maid but fain would be a bride. . . .
> *Bas.*   He levels fair that by his side
>   Lays at night his lovely bride.
> *Cho.*   Sing Io, Hymen! Io, Io, Hymen!

This is clearly inspired by the debate on the advantages of matronhood over maidenhood, *Carm.* lxii *passim.* For the chorus, see *Carm.* lxi., 144-145.
> O Hymen Hymenaee io,
> O Hymen Hymenaee.

(13)   *Ibid.* (Bullen, p. 157):
> Virginity is a voluntary power
> Free from constraint, even like an untouched flower
> Meet to be gathered when 'tis throughly blown.

See *Carm.* lxii, 39-45:
> Ut flos in saeptis secretus nascitur hortis. . .
> Sic virgo, dum intacta manet, dum cara suis est.

(14)   *Ibid.* (Bullen, p. 169-170):
> Hesperus *loquitur:*
> I, that wished evening star, must now make way
> To Hymen's rights much wronged by my delay.

For a probable source see *Carm.* lxii, 1-2;
> Vesper adest: iuvenes, consurgite: Vesper Olympo
> Exspectata diu vix tandem lumina tollit.

(15)   *Ibid.* (Bullen, p. 170)
> 1.   Of all the stars which is the kindest
>   To a loving Bride?
> 2.   Hesperus when in the west
>   He doth day from night divide.

  1. What message can be more respected
    Than that which tells wished joys shall be effected?
  2. Do not brides watch the evening star?
  1. O they can discern it far. . .

  Cho. Hesperus, since you all stars excel
     In bridal kindness, kindly farewell, farewell.
See *Carm.* lxii, 26-30:
  Hespere, qui caelo lucet iucundior ignis?
  Qui desponsa tua firmes connubia flamma,
  Quae pepigere viri, pepigerunt ante parentes.
  Nec iunxere prius quam se tuus extulit ardor.
  Quid datur a divis felici optatius hora?

  (16) In the *Masque at the Marriage of the Earl of Somerset* Campion introduces the Fates to sing the happiness of the bride and bridegroom; he acknowledges his indebtedness to Catullus in his description of his characters (Bullen, p. 222):
    Next, came the three Destinies, in long robes of white taffeta like aged women, with garlands of Narcissus flowers on their heads; and in their left hands they carried distaffs according to the descriptions of Plato and Catullus.....
See *Carm.* lxiv, 306-311:
  Veridicos Parcae coeperunt edere cantus,
  His corpus tremulum complectens undique vestis
  Candida purpurea talos incinxerat ora,
  At roseae niveo residebant vertice vittae,
  Aeternumque manus carpebant rite laborem.
  Laeva colum molli lana retinebat amictum.
  The whole conception of the concluding scene of the Masque seems to have been drawn from Catullus; verbal likeness, so far as I can discover, there is little or none, but Campion shows clearly, near the very end of the Masque, that he has had Catullus largely in mind (Bullen, p. 227):
  All blessings which the Fates prophetic sung
  At Peleus' nuptials, and whatever tongue
  Can figure more, this night, and aye betide
  The honored bridegroom and the honored bride.
See *Carm.* lxiv, 303-383.

  (17) From *Observations on the Art of English Poetry*, the sixth epigram (Bullen, p. 251):
  What though Harry brags, let him be noble;
  Noble Harry hath not half a noble.
This, to my mind, has a very considerable likeness to *Carm.* xxiv, 7-10:
  "Quid? Non est homo bellus?" inquies. Est:
  Sed bello huic neque servus est neque arca.
  Hoc tu quam libet abice elevaque:
  Nec servum tamen ille habet neque arcam.

So much for what I consider the direct influence of Catullus upon Campion, yet, to my mind, the real influence of the Latin poet is far greater and more pervasive. Again and again in reading Campion I have thought, "These words of Campion's are not close to those of Catullus, but he is thinking as Catullus thought, and the love of which he sings, lighter, flimsier, often, indeed, artificial as it is, makes him speak very much as Catullus spoke." It is especially in Campion's expressions of distrust of his lady and in his consequent sorrow that this likeness is most apparent:

> Shall then a traitorous kiss or a smile
> All my delights unhappily beguile?
> Shall the vow of feigned love receive so rich regard,
> When true service dies neglected, and wants his due reward?

This is in the manner of Catullus when Catullus is recriminating. His love is in its various stages like that of the Latin poet; he promises undying affection:

> Yet truth can tell my heart is hers,
>   And her will I adore;
> And from that love when I depart,
>   Let heaven view me no more!
>   (Bullen, p. 68)

He knows that his mistress is deceiving him, yet he craves a happy ignorance:

> Veil, Love, mine eyes! O hide from me
>   The plagues that charge the curious mind!
> If beauty private will not be,
>   Suffice it yet that she proves kind.
> Who can usurp heaven's light alone?
> Stars were not made to shine on one.
>   (Bullen, p. 113)

He feels deeply the wrong his mistress does his love:

> O bitter grief! that exile is become
> Reward for faith, and pity deaf and dumb!
>   (Bullen, p. 84)

But he sees, as Catullus foresaw, retribution for the fair false one:

> Where are all thy beauties now, all hearts enchaining?
> Whither are thy flatterers gone with all their feigning?
> All fled! and thou alone still here remaining.
>   (Bullen, p. 48)

None of these would one venture to ascribe to the direct influence of Catullus, but surely the feeling, the motivation is the same. In many ways, in my estimation, Campion is the nearest to Catullus of the poets concerned in this consideration; certainly, as I have said before, if he yields to any one, he yields only to Herrick.

SIR WALTER RALEIGH
(1552-1618)

SIR HENRY WOTTON
(1568-1639)

Sir Walter Raleigh's acquaintance with the classic authors was very considerable, as the translations from the Latin poets among his poems attest—Claudian, Vergil, Ovid, Ausonius—short passages of these and other poets he translated into English. I can find but one trace of Catullus; in Book I, Chapter II of the *History of the World* we have the verses:

> The sun may set and rise;
> But we, contrariwise,
> Sleep after our short light
> One everlasting night.

This is a translation of *Carm.* v. 4-6, the familiar *Soles occidere et redire possunt.*

There seems to be only one possible reference to Catullus among the poems of Sir Henry Wotton: in the poem beginning *O faithless world* (Hannah's edition, p. 87), we find the verses:

> Why was she born to please? or I to trust
>   Words writ in dust?
> Suffering my eyes to govern my despair,
>   My pain for air.

This may be an echo of *Carm.* lxx, 3-4:

> . . . Mulier cupido quod dicit amanti
>   In vento et rapida scribere oportet aqua.

SAMUEL DANIEL
(1562-1619)

The influence of Catullus upon Daniel is clear and marked. Daniel was, of course, not primarily, but only incidentally, a lyrist: the great bulk of his work lies in the interminable *Histories*. But when he did turn to the writing of lyrics he wrote with a clearness and grace which had much of the classical in them. The quotations which follow show that Daniel used his great source with judgment and taste; Catullus is never dishonored in the imitation. The first quotation is, to my mind, an unusually graceful adaptation of the *Vivamus, mea Lesbia*. The long *Complaint of Rosamond*, while not strictly a lyric in form, is essentially lyrical in temper, and, as such, falls under the liberal definition of "lyrical" which I suggested for our use in the *Introduction*. Strangely enough, the most characteristically lyric portion of Daniel's work, the sonnet sequence to Delia, contains, so far as I can discover, no reference to Catullus at all. The reason may be simple enough: where Daniel was most lyrical he was least imitative.

(1)   From *A Pastoral* (Chalmers, III, p. 549):
> Let's love—this life of ours
> Can make no truce with Time that all devours.
> Let's love—the Sun doth set, and rise again;
> But when as our short light
> Comes once to set, it makes eternal night.

See *Carm*. v, 1 and 4-6:
> Vivamus, mea Lesbia, atque amemus. . .
> Soles occidere et redire possunt:
> Nobis, cum semel occidit brevis lux,
> Nox est perpetua una dormienda.

(2)   From *The Complaint of Rosamond*, (Chalmers, III, p. 563):
> Com'd was the Night (mother of Sleep and Fear)
> That with her sable mantle friendly covers
> The sweet stoll'n sport of joyful meeting lovers.

See *Carm*. vii, 7-8, for a possible but far from certain source:
> Aut quam sidera multa, cum tacet nox,
> Furtivos hominum vident amores.

and *Carm*. lxviii, 145:
> Sed furtiva dedit mira munuscula nocte.

(3)   *Ibid.* (Chalmers, III, p. 565):
> "And poor distressed Rosamond," said I,
> "Is this thy glory got, to die forlorn
> In deserts where no ear can hear thee mourn?"

See *Carm*. lxiv, 169-170:
> Sed nimis insultans extremo tempore saeva
> Fors etiam nostris invidit questibus auris.

(4)   *Ibid.* (Chalmers, III, p. 565):
>   Condole thee here, clad all in black despair,
>   With silence only, and a dying bed;
>   Thou that of late, so flourishing, so fair,
>   Didst glorious live, admir'd and honoured:
>   And now from friends, from succor hither led,
>   Art made a spoil to lust, to wrath, to death,
>   And in disgrace, forced here to yield thy breath.

See *Carm.* lxiv, where a like contrast is drawn between Ariadne before her betrayal by Theseus, 86-88:

>   . . . Virgo
>   Regia, quam suavis exspirans castus odores
>   Lectulus in molli complexu matris alebat;

and her deserted state after her betrayal, 177-185:

>   Nam quo me referam? quali spe perdita nitor? . . .
>   An patris auxilium sperem? . . .
>   Coniugis an fido consoler memet amore,
>   Quine fugit lentos incurvans gurgite remos? . . .
>   Nulla fugae ratio, nulla spes: omnia muta,
>   Omnia sunt deserta, ostentant omnia letum.

The verbal resemblances of this *Complaint of Rosamond* to the complaint of the deserted Ariadne are considerable, but, to my mind, these resemblances in wording do not tell the entire story; the influence of Catullus's great lyrical outburst permeates much of *Rosamond* in a way less easily analyzable and yet not less real than the actual verbal resemblances pointed out.

(5)   *Ibid.* (Chalmers, III, p. 566):
>   Striving to tell his woes, words would not come;
>   For light cares speak, when mighty griefs are dumb.

Perhaps an echo, though I hazard this only as a suggestion, of *Carm.* lxv, 3-4:
>   Non potis est dulcis Musarum expromere fetus
>   Mens animi: tantis fluctuat ipsa malis.

(6)   *Ibid.* (Chalmers, III, p. 566):
>   He draws him near my body to behold it;
>   And as the vine married unto the elm,
>   With strict embraces, so doth he infold it.

See *Carm.* lxii, 49, 54:
>   Ut vidua in nudo vitis quae nascitur arvo. . .
>   . . . Si forte eadem est ulmo coniuncta marito. . . .

(7)   From the *Prologue of Hymen's Triumph* (Chalmers, III, p. 571):
>   In this disguise and pastoral attire,
>   Without my saffron robe, without my torch,
>   Or rather ensigns of my duty,
>   I Hymen am come hither secretly.

See *Carm*. lxi, 8, 15:

> Flammeum cape, laetus huc. . .
> Pineam quate taedam.

A further evidence of Daniel's knowledge of Catullus we may see in his *Defence of Rhyme:*

(8)   From the *Defence of Rhyme* (Chalmers, III, p. 559):

> For there is not the simplest writer that will ever tell himself he doth ill, but as if he were the parasite only to sooth his own doings, persuades him that his lines cannot but please others, which so much delight himself:

> > Suffenus est quisque sibi—neque idem unquam
> > Aeque est beatus, ac poema cum scribit,
> > Tam gaudet in se tamque se ipse miratur.

The name "Suffenus" is that of one of the bad poets whom Catullus decries and ridicules; from "neque idem" on, the three lines are quoted from *Carm*. xxii, 15-17. "Suffenus est quisque sibi" paraphrases xxii, *Carm*. 18-20:

> > — Neque est quisquam
> > Quem non in aliqua re videre Suffenum
> > Possis.

SIR JOHN DAVIES
(1569-1626)

The influence of Catullus upon Davies is comparatively slight. Davies's most characteristic poems are, unquestionably, the *Nosce Teipsum* and the *Orchestra*, poems essentially didactic and philosophical in nature rather than lyrical and passionate. That Davies knew Catullus, our quotations, I think, make sufficiently clear; but his knowledge of the Latin poet seems to be that of an educated man to whose memory there come floating, as occasion demands, fragments of an author browsed through in youth, and all but forgotten until the specific need arises. Surely Catullus, from the quotations which follow, does not appear greatly to have moulded Davies's poetical powers, as he does clearly appear to have done in the case of Jonson or Campion or Herrick. In Davies we have but cold recollections of learning assimilated, not true poetry in one language aroused by loving reading of true poetry in another.

(1) From the *Dedication to Orchestra, addressed to Mr. Richard Martin* (Grosart, I, p. 159):

> To whom shall I this dancing poem send,
> This sudden, rash, half-capreol of my wit?
> To you, first mover and sole cause of it,
> Mine-own-selves better half, my dearest friend.

This seems modeled on Catullus's dedication, *Carm.* i, 1-4:

> Cui dono lepidum novum libellum
> Arido modo pumice expolitum?
> Corneli, tibi; namque tu solebas
> Meas esse aliquid putare nugas.

(2) From *A Contention Betwixt a Wife, a Widdow, and a Maide,* (Grosart, II, p. 72 ff.):

> Wife: The wife is like a fair supported vine.
> Widow: So was the widow, but now stands alone:
>   For being grown strong, she needs not to incline.
> Maid: Maids, like the earth, supported are of none.
>   . . . .
> Widow: Then what's a virgin but a fruitless bay?
> Maid: And what's a widow but a rose-less briar?
>   And what are wives, but woodbinds which decay
>   The stately oaks by which themselves aspire?
>   . . . .
> Wife: The wife is like a fair manurèd field;
> Widow: The widow once was such, but now doth rest.
> Maid: The maid, like Paradise, undrest, untill'd,
>   Bears crops of native virtue in her breast.

The similes used in this controversy are, in the main, those used in the match between the youths and the maidens, *Carm.* lxii. There, 39, the maids declare that a virgin is

> Ut flos in saeptis secretus nascitur hortis,

while the youths, 49-50, 56, maintain that:

> Ut vidua in nudo vitis quae nascitur arvo
> Nunquam se extollit, nunquam mitem educat uvam. . .
> Sic virgo, dum intacta manet, dum inculta senescit.

The Latin passages are found quoted in full in the chapter on Jonson, articles 16 and 17. The Catullian influence is, to my mind, clear in this poem of Davies, but not sufficiently close verbally to warrant my quoting the Latin at length.

(3)   *Allusion to Theseus' voyage to Crete against the Minotaure:* (Grosart, II, p. 102):

> My love is sail'd against dislike to fight,
> Which like vile monster, threatens his decay. . .

It is possible that for the idea of this forced and unnatural sonnet Davies may be indebted to the episode of Theseus and Ariadne in *Carm.* lxiv, yet that, of course, is but one of many possible sources.

(4)   From *On the Death of Lord Chancellor Ellesmere's Second Wife in 1599* (Grosart, II, p. 112):

> My prop is fallen, and quenchèd is my light:
> But th' Elm may stand, when wither'd is the vine.

If it be true, as I believe it is, that Davies drew on Catullus in his verses quoted above (2), then this simile may well be reminiscent of the passage there indicated, *Carm.* lxii, 54:

> At si forte eadem [vitis] est ulmo coniuncta marito. . .

The *Epigrammes* of Sir John Davies present something of a difficulty; Harrington believes that in them Davies is "imitating the scurrilous attacks of the worst Catullian epigrams, and the odious personal characteristics of the notorious Ameana, Rufus, Gellius, and Aemilius are predicated of later objects of poetic spleen."[1] Undoubtedly they are much in the manner of Catullus's coarser poems; even when they have no other quality in common with Catullus's epigrams, they have a truly Catullian indelicacy. They are sharp, pungent bits of invective, dealing in large part with the subjects Catullus belabored, vice, personal defects, affectations, and the like, but direct verbal influence does not appear. The nearest resemblance to Catullus is found in those epigrams which Davies addresses to women he dislikes. Thus:

(5)   Epigram 11, *In Gellam* (Grosart, II, p. 15):

> Gella, if thou dost love thy self, take heed,
> Lest thou my rimes unto thy lover read;
> For straight thou grin'st and then thy lover seeth
> Thy canker-eaten gums and rotten teeth.

---

1   Harrington, *op. cit.*, p. 159.

and

    (6)   Epigram 26, *In Gellam* (Grosart, II, p. 26):

> If Gella's beauty be examinèd,
> She hath a dull, dead eye, a saddle nose,
> And ill-shap't face, with morphew over-spread,
> And rotten teeth, which she in laughing shows;
> Briefly, she is the filthiest wench in town,
> Of all that do the art of whoring use. . .

These, indeed, are in the Catullian manner; see *Carm.* xliii, 1-5:

> Salve, nec minimo puella naso,
> Nec bello pede nec nigris ocellis,
> Nec longis digitis nec ore sicco,
> Nec sane nimis elegante lingua,
> Decoctoris amica Formiani. . .

and xli, 1-3:

> Ameana puella defututa
> Tota milia me decem poposcit,
> Ista turpiculo puella naso. . .

Davies, like Catullus, directs epigrams against affectations in speech (*In Macrum*, Ep. 15; see *Carm.* lxxxiv); against indiscriminate vice (*In Sillam*, Ep. 28; see, for one example, *Carm.* lvii); and against bad poets, or what he considered bad poets (*In Dacum*, Ep. 30; see, for one example, *Carm.* xxii). But one cannot, with proper regard for the facts, read the influence of Catullus into Davies's epigrams; if he had the Latin poet in mind at all, he had but such a remembrance of his epigrams as would stay with him after a single perusal; surely of no one epigram can it be said that it is modeled upon an epigram of Catullus.

MICHAEL DRAYTON
(1563-1631)

I am not at all sure that Drayton was even in the least familiar with Catullus. Indeed, either he knew the Latin poet not at all or his knowledge of Latin literary history was most elementary; for in his first Ode, *To Himself, and the Harp*, he speaks of

—Him that Rome did grace
Whose airs we all embrace,
   That scarcely found his peer,
Nor giveth Phoebus place
   For strokes divinely clear,

and informs us, in his note, that he is referring to "Horace, first of the Romans in that kind."[1] The question indeed arises whether he means "first in merit" or "first in order of time"; if he means "first in time" it would seem almost certain that he had no direct knowledge of Catullus at all. There are, so far as I can discover, only two possible suggestions of Catullus in Drayton's lyrical poetry:

(1)   In the *Ninth Eclogue* (Chalmers, IV, p. 444):
Rowland: And said that Ariadne's crown
Chorus: With these compar'd,
           The gods should not regard
           Nor Berenice's hair.

This may be a reference to the *Coma Berenices*, *Carm.* lxvi, but Drayton might well have come upon the allusion in a poet of his own day, Jonson or Chapman, for example.

(2)   In the *Eighth Nymphal* (Chalmers, IV, p. 464) there is mention of the scattering of nuts at a wedding:

When about the room we ramble,
Scatter nuts and for them scramble.

The chief source for any mention of this practice is *Carm.* lxi, 128: *Nec nuces pueris neget*, etc., but Vergil has a similar allusion (*Eclogues*, VIII, 29): *Tibi ducitur uxor; Sparge, marite, nuces.*

---

1   Chalmers, *English Poets*, IV, p. 423.

JOHN DONNE
(1573-1631)

In Donne, as I have had occasion to say in the *Introduction* to these studies, the classical influence is very small; indeed, he seemed to set himself resolutely against the prevailing habit of copious classical allusion. For this Carew praised him most enthusiastically, maintaining that he had freed English verse from cheapness:

> Whatsoever wrong
> By ours was done the Greek and Latin tongue
> Thou hast redeem'd, and open'd us a mine
> Of rich and pregnant fancy; drawn a line
> Of masculine expression, which, had good
> Old Orpheus seen, or all the ancient brood
> Our superstitious fools admire, and hold
> Their lead more precious than thy burnish'd gold
> Thou hadst been their exchequer, and no more
> They in each other's dung had search'd for ore;

now that the great Donne is dead, went on Carew, bad poets, "libertines in poetry"

> ...Will recall the goodly exiled train
> Of gods and goddesses, which in thy just reign
> Was banish'd nobler poems; now with these,
> The silenc'd tales i' th' Metamorphoses
> Shall stuff their lines, and swell the windy page.[1]

Carew undoubtedly goes too far both in condemning the classicists and in praising Donne for his freedom from classical influence, but his lines are, to my mind, important for anyone considering the influence of the ancients upon Donne's poetry. Donne was a man who stood alone in his verse; his faults and his virtues are his own; he does not buttress himself with the stolen beauties of others. "It is clear," says Professor Grierson, "that he knew the classical poets, but there are few specific allusions. Ovid, Horace, and Juvenal one can trace, not any other with certainty, nor in his sermons do references to Virgil, Horace, or other poets abound."[2] So it was that "what he wanted as a poet were just the two essentials of 'classical' poetry—smoothness of verse and dignity of expression."[3] There is in his verse, again to quote Professor Grierson, "far less ... of the superficial evidence of classical learning with which the poetry of the 'University Wits' abounds, pastoral and mythological imagery. ... The place of the

> goodly exiled train
> Of gods and goddesses

is taken by images drawn from all the sciences of the day, from the definitions and the distinctions of the Schoolmen, from the travels and speculations of the new age,

---

1 *Poems of Thomas Carew*, edited by Arthur Vincent, p. 101-102.
2 H. J. C. Grierson, *Donne's Poetical Works*, II, p. 2.
3 *Ibid.*, p. vii.

and . . . . from the experiences of everyday life."[4] Professor Grierson then goes on to point out that there is another side to the matter, in that "there is no poet the spirit of whose love-poetry is so classical, so penetrated with the sensual, realistic, scornful tone of the Latin lyric and elegiac poets,"[5] and in illumination of this he draws a rather close parallel between Donne and the Ovid of the *Amores*.

That there is a considerable affinity between the love-poetry of Donne and Catullus, Professor Grierson points out also—"It is only in the fragments of Sappho, the lyrics of Catullus, and the songs of Burns that one will find the sheer joy of loving and being loved expressed in the same direct and simple language as in some of Donne's songs."[6] But, by and large, there is a very great difference between Catullus's simple, clear, passionate expression of his love, and Donne's subtle, involved, too often turbid verse. It is, to my mind, more often in his sadder moments, rather than when the surge of passion is sweeping over him, that Donne approaches nearest to Catullus. Take, for example, that exquisite opening stanza of *The Relique* (Grierson, I, p. 62):

> When my grave is broke up again
> Some second guest to entertain,
> (For graves have learn'd that woman-head
> To be to more than one a bed)
>   And he that digs it, spies
> A bracelet of bright hair about the bone,
>   Will he not let us alone,
> And think that there a loving couple lies,
> Who thought that this device might be some way
> To make their souls, at the last busy day,
> Meet at this grave, and make a little stay?

Had Catullus been a Christian, and had Lesbia died while he still thought her faithful, he would, I think, have sung as Donne here sings. And Catullus, grown contemplative, weary of life and loving, could not have surpassed the magnificent closing lines of *The Autumnall* (Grierson, I, p. 94):

> I hate extremes; yet I had rather stay
>   With tombs, than cradles, to wear out a day.
> Since such love's natural lation is, may still
>   My love descend, and journey down the hill,
> Not panting after growing beauties, so,
>   I shall ebb out with them, who home-ward go.

But it is not too profitable, perhaps, to speculate on the spiritual kinship of two poets so divorced in time and manner as Donne and Catullus. There is no certainty that Donne knew Catullus at all; the testimony of silence is against his having done so; on the other hand, it is very probable that among the "1400 authors" of whom "he left the resultances. . . most of them abridged and analysed with his own hand,"[7] Catullus may have found a place. The *Epithalamions*, where, first of all,

---

4   *Ibid.*, p. xxxviii.
5   *Ibid.*, p. xxxix.
6   *Ibid.*, pp. xlii-xliii.
7   Izaac Walton, *The Life of Dr. John Donne* (Ed. 1858, p. 68).

one looks for evidences of Catullian influence in this period, are almost without direct or indirect traces of Catullus, though as Professor Grierson remarks, Donne comes nearer to Spenser in his treatment of this theme than in any other kind,[8] and Spenser was profoundly influenced by Catullus. The examples which follow are all of them far from certain and assured; they have likenesses to various passages in Catullus, but in no one of them can one be sure of the direct influence of the Latin poet.

(1) From *The Message* (Grierson, I, p. 43):
> Yet send me back my heart and eyes,
> That I may know, and see thy lies,
> And may laugh and joy, when thou
>   Art in anguish
>   And dost languish
>   For some one
>   That will none,
> Or prove as false as thou art now.

This bears a certain resemblance to Catullus's prediction of a joyless future for his faithless mistress, *Carm.* viii, 12-19, already quoted:

> At tu dolebis, cum rogaberis nulla.
> Scelesta, vae te! quae tibi manet vita? etc.

(2) From *A Nocturnall upon S. Lucies day* (Grierson, I, p. 45):
> If I an ordinary nothing were,
> As shadow, a light, and body must be here.
> *But I am None; nor will my Sun renew.*
> You lovers, for whose sake, the lesser Sun
>   At this time to the Goat is run
>   To fetch new lust, and give it you,
>   Enjoy your summer all.

This is, of course, the familiar theme of *Carm.* v,

> Soles occidere et redire possunt;

note especially the italicized line.

(3) From *Elegie VIII, The Comparison* (Grierson, I, 90-92):
> As the sweet sweat of roses in a still,
> As that which from chaf'd muskats' pores doth trill,
> As the almighty balm of th' early East,
> Such are the sweat drops of my Mistris' breast. . .
> Rank sweaty froth thy Mistress's brow defiles,
> Like spermatic issue of ripe menstruous boils. . .
> Leave her, and I will leave comparing thus,
> She, and comparisons are odious.

This is much in the manner of Catullus's denunciations of rival beauties, who would compare themselves with Lesbia; see, for example, *Carm.* xliii:

8   Grierson, *Ibid.*, II, pp. 91-2.

Salve, nec minimo puella naso
Nec bello pede nec nigris ocellis
Nec longis digitis nec ore sicco,
Nec sane nimis elegante lingua,
Decoctoris amica Formiani.
Ten Provincia narrat esse bellam?
Tecum Lesbia nostra comparatur?
O saeclum insapiens et infacetum!

The resemblance is indubitably present, but Donne far surpasses in coarseness the Latin poet. He had no need of help to be foul.

(4)   From *Elegie XII, His Parting from Her* (Grierson, I, p. 100-101):
Oh Love, that fire and darkness should be mixt,
Or to thy triumphs so strange torments fixt?. . . .
. . . Have we left undone some mutual rite
Through holy fear, that merits thy despite?

The last two lines are reminiscent of *Carm.* lxviii, 75-77, 79-80:
—Domum
Inceptam frustra, nondum cum sanguine sacro
    Hostia caelestis pacificasset eros. . . .
Quam ieiuna pium desideret ara cruorem,
    Docta est amisso Laodamia viro.

(5)   *Ibid.*, (Grierson, I, p. 102):
Let our arms clasp like Ivy, and our fear
Freeze us together, that we may stick here.

A familiar Catullian simile (see *Carm.* lxi, 106-109), but Donne might very well have used it had he never heard of Catullus.

(6)   From *Upon Mr. Thomas Coryat's Crudities* (Grierson, I, p. 173):
The East sends hither her deliciousness;
And thy leaves must embrace what comes from thence,
The Myrrh, the Pepper, and the Frankincense. . . .
        . . . It thy leaves do then
Convey these wares in parcels unto men. . . .

This bears a certain resemblance to the lines in which Catullus predicts a like fate for a bad poet; see *Carm.* xcv, 7-8:
At Volusi annales Paduam morientur ad ipsam
    Et laxas scombris saepe dabunt tunicas.

(7)   From *Epithalamion Made at Lincoln's Inn* (Grierson, I, p. 142):
All elder claims, and all cold barrenness,
All yielding to new loves be far for ever,
    Which might these two dissever.

For a parallel passage, see *Carm.* lxi, 146-148:
Scimus haec tibi quae licent
Sola cognita: sed marito
Ista non eadem licent.

(8) *Ibid.*:
> Oh winter days bring much delight,
> Nor for themselves, but for they soon bring night.

For a probable influence, see *Carm.* lxviii, 81-83:
> Coniugis ante coacta novi dimittere collum
> Quam veniens una atque altera rursus hiems
> Noctibus in longis avidum saturasset amorem.

(9) From *Love's Deitie* (Grierson, I, p. 54):
> I long to talk with some old lover's ghost
>   Who died before the god of Love was born;
> I cannot think that he, who then lov'd most,
>   Sunk so low, as to love one which did scorn.
> But since this god produc'd a destiny,
> And that vice-nature, custom, lets it be:
>   I must love her that loves not me.

"Here," says Mr. Gosse, "the note is as the note of Catullus," and he quotes *Carm.* lxxxv:
> Odi et amo. Quare id faciam fortasse requiris.
>   Nescio, sed fieri sentio et excrucior.[9]

But even here there is not the least certainty of direct influence.

The fifteenth elegy, *The Expostulation*, is claimed for Donne by all the editors of his poetry, including the most recent, Professor Grierson of the University of Edinburgh; it is claimed also by the editors of Jonson. I have had the very great advantage of discussing at length the authorship of this poem with Professor Grierson. He acknowledged that the quotations which I have given above were far from conclusive in establishing Donne's acquaintance with Catullus, and that *The Expostulation* shows very clear evidences of a fairly intimate acquaintance with the Latin poet. He still holds, however, that *The Expostulation* is Donne's. This is certain, that if Donne wrote *The Expostulation* he was well acquainted with Catullus, and that nothing else in his poems indicates clearly such an acquaintance. I have, therefore, in this consideration dealt with *The Expostulation* as one of Jonson's poems; for the traces of a Catullian influence in it, see JONSON, (5), (6), and (7). I do not attempt to pass upon the authorship of the poem; for interesting discussions of this question, see *Did Jonson Write the Expostulation?*, by M. L. Wilder, in the *Modern Language Review*, Vol. XXI, pp. 431-435; Herford and Simpson's *Ben Jonson*, II, pp. 383-4; and Professor W. D. Briggs's review of the book just named, in *Modern Language Notes*, Vol. XLII, pp. 409-10. I have added materially to the evidences of a Catullian influence in the poem.

---

9 Gosse, *Life and Letters of John Donne*, I, p. 72.

GEORGE HERBERT
(1593-1633)

As was to be expected, no trace of a Catullian influence appears in the poems of George Herbert. They are, as they have survived, almost wholly religious in nature; yet he owns to lighter verses in his youth. Thus, in *The Convert* (Grosart, p. 261), he renounces his earlier verse:

> My verse that oft with foolish lays,
> With vows and rants and senseless praise
> Frail Beauty's charms to heav'n did raise,
>   Henceforth shall only pierce the skies
>   In penitential cries.

He tells us of the diffidence with which he turned from secular verse (*The Priesthood*, Grosart, p. 202):

> But thou art fire, sacred and hallow'd fire,
> And I but earth and clay; should I presume
> To wear thy habit, the severe attire
> My slender compositions might consume.

But finally he gives himself to religion and religious poetry with all his heart, marvelling at the prevalence of secular verse (*Sonnet*, Grosart, p. 277):

>   Doth Poetry
> Wear Venus' livery, only serve her turn?
> Why are not sonnets made of Thee, and lays
> Upon thy altar burnt?

GEORGE CHAPMAN
(1559-1634)

Chapman's genius was not primarily lyrical; the great μεταφράστης of Homer was too diffuse, too flood-like in his verse-making, to succeed greatly, or to try to succeed, in lyric poetry. "Chapman, laborious translator and dramatist, poet of difficult epicedes and occasional verses. . . . could write a lyric with admirable success, though Chapman, for the most part, stood aloof from so trivial an employment of the divine gift of poetry."[1] Chapman was too thorough a classicist not to know his Catullus thoroughly, but between the English translator and dramatist and the Latin lyrist there lay too wide an abyss of mood, manner, and matter for Catullus to exert any real influence upon Chapman. The traces of Catullus are there, but they are of no very great importance in the vast bulk of Chapman's verse. I have instanced nine such passages.

(1)   From *Hero and Leander*, the *Epithalamion Teratos* (*Minor Poems and Translations*, p. 87):

> The evening star I see:
>   Rise, youths, the evening star
>   Helps Love to summon war;
> Both now embracing be.
>
> Rise, youths, Love's rite claims more than banquets, rise. . .
> Now Love in Night, and Night in Love exhorts
> Courtship and dances: all your parts employ,
> And suit Night's rich expansure with your joy.
> Love paints his longings in sweet virgins' eyes:
> Rise, youths, Love's rite claims more than banquets; rise.

See *Carm.* lxii, 1-4:

> Vesper adest: iuvenes, consurgite: Vesper Olympo
> Exspectata diu vix tandem lumina tollit.
> Surgere iam tempus, iam pinguis linquere mensas;
> Iam veniet virgo, iam dicetur hymenaeus.

(2)   *Ibid.*:

> Rise, virgins, let fair nuptial loves enfold
> Your fruitless breasts: the maidenheads ye hold
> Are not your own alone, but parted are;
> Part in disposing them your parents share,
> And that a third part is; so must ye save
> Your loves a third, and you your thirds must have.
> Love paints his longings in sweet virgins' eyes:
> Rise, youths, Love's rite claims more than banquets; rise.

---

1   Schelling, *The English Lyric*, p. 70.

See *Carm.* lxii, 59, 62-65:

>Et tu ne pugna cum tali coniuge, virgo. . .
>Virginitas non tota tua est, ex parte parentum est:
>Tertia pars patri, pars est data tertia matri,
>Tertia sola tua est. Noli pugnare duobus,
>Qui genero sua iura simul cum dote dederunt.

(3)   From *A Good Woman* (*Minor Poems and Translations*, p. 151):
>When a just husband's right he would enjoy,
>She neither flies him, nor with moods is coy.

This may be an echo of *Carm.* lxi, 151-153:

>Nupta, tu quoque quae tuus
>Vir petet cave ne neges,
>Ni petitum aliunde eat.

(4)   From *A Hymn to Hymen for the Most Time-fitted Nuptials of the Princess Elizabeth* (*M. P. a. T.*, pp. 176-177):
>Sing, sing a rapture to all nuptial ears,
>Bright Hymen's torches, drunk up Parcae's tears,
>Sweet Hymen, Hymen, mightiest of Gods,
>Atoning of all-taming blood the odds.

See *Carm.* lxi, 64-65:

>Quis huic deo
>Comparier ausit?

(5)   *Ibid.*:
>The whole court Iö sings: Iö the air:
>Iö the floods, and fields: Iö most fair,
>Most sweet, most happy Hymen; come: away.

See *Carm.* lxi, 123-125:

>Ite, concinite in modum
>'O Hymen Hymenaee io,
>O Hymen Hymenaee.'

(6)   *Ibid.*:
>And, as the tender hyacinth, that grows
>Where Phoebus most his golden beams bestows,
>Is propt with care; is water'd every hour,
>The sweet winds adding their increasing power. . .
>So, of a virgin, high, and richly kept,
>The grace and sweetness full grown must be reap'd.

See *Carm.* lxi, 91-93:

>Talis in vario solet
>Divitis domini hortulo
>Stare flos hyacinthus. . .

(7)   From *Andromeda Liberta* (*M. P. a. T.*, pp. 191-192):
>   And said they [the Fates] sung verse, that posterity
>   In no age should reprove for perfidy.

See *Carm.* lxiv, 320-322:
>   Haec tum clarisona, vellentes vellera, voce
>   Talia divino fuderunt carmine fata,
>   Carmine, perfidiae quod post nulla arguet aetas.

(8)   The *Parcarum Epithalamion* (*M. P. a. T.*, pp. 191-192) in *Andromeda Liberta* is obviously inspired by the Songs of the Fates in Catullus, *Carm.* lxiv, 323-381, and is modeled upon it. The refrain:
>   Haste you that guide the web, haste, spindles, haste,

is a translation of Catullus's refrain:
>   Currite, ducentes subtegmina, currite, fusi.

The influence of Catullus is most marked in the form of the *Epithalamion*; the verbal likeness is comparatively slight, save in the first stanza:
>   O you, this Kingdom's glory that shall be
>   Parents to so renown'd a progeny
>   As earth shall envy and heaven glory in,
>   Accept of their lives' threads which Fate shall spin,
>   Their true-spoke oracle, and live to see
>   Your son's sons enter such a progeny,
>   As to the last times of the world shall last.
>   *Haste you that guide the web, haste, spindles, haste.*

See *Carm.* lxiv, 325-326, and 338-341:
>   Accipe quod laeta tibi pandunt luce sorores,
>   Veridicum oraculum. . .
>   Nascetur vobis expers terroris Achilles,
>   Hostibus haud tergo, sed forti pectore notus,
>   Qui persaepe vago victor certamine cursus
>   Flammea praevertet celeris vestigia cervae.
>   Currite ducentes subtegmina, currite, fusi.

(9)   From *Verses Appended to the Translation of The Odyssey* (*M. P. a. T.*, p. 253):
>   His trash, by foolish Fame brought now, from hence
>   Given to serve mackarel forth, and frankincense.

See *Carm.* xcv, 7-8:
>   At Volusi annales Paduam morientur ad ipsam
>   Et laxas scombris saepe dabunt tunicas.

THE SONG BOOKS
(1588-1632)

We may well examine the song books at this point, the end of the period in which they flourished. As a whole, they fail to show any considerable Catullian influence, or, indeed, anything but a rather perfunctory knowledge and use of certain of the classical poets. Such references as one does find are, as a rule, most conventional; I open at random to Orlando Gibbon's *The First Set of Madrigals and Motets*, and take the first stanza that happens to meet my eye, the 13th:

> Lais now old, that erst attempting lass,
> To goddess Venus consecrates her glass;
> For she herself hath now no use of one,
> No dimpled cheeks hath she to gaze upon.
> She cannot see her springtime damask grace,
> Nor dare she look upon her winter face.

Here Lais is a classical name chosen at random, the reference to Venus of the most conventional kind, and the thought itself, while paralleled in Horace, for example, is not attributable to any of the older poets.

I have examined the song books of the following authors and have found in them nothing to indicate acquaintance with Catullus (I follow the division into "Madrigalists" and "Lutenists" made by Mr. E. H. Fellowes in his very valuable collection, *English Madrigal Verse*):

The Madrigalists:

Richard Alison	1606
Thomas Bateson	1604, 1618
John Bennet	1599
William Byrd	1588, 1589, 1611
Richard Carlton	1601
Michael East	1604, 1606, 1610, 1619, 1624
John Farmer	1599
Giles Farnaby	1598
Orlando Gibbons	1612
John Hilton	1627
William Holborne	1597
Robert Jones	1607
George Kirbye	1597
Henry Lichfild	1613
Thomas Morley	1593, 1594, 1595, 1595, 1597, 1601
John Mundy	1594
Martin Peerson	1620, 1630
Francis Pilkington	1613, 1624
Thomas Ravenscroft	1614
Thomas Vautor	1619
Thomas Tomkins	1622
John Ward	1613

Thomas Weelkes_____1597, 1598, 1600, 1600, 1608
John Wilbye_____1598, 1609
Harry Youll_____1608

The Lutenists:
John Attey_____1622
William Barley_____1596
Michael Cavendish_____1598
John Cooper_____1606, 1613
John Danyel_____1606
Robert Dowland_____1610
Thomas Ford_____1607
Thomas Greaves _____1604
Tobias Hume_____1605, 1607
George Mason_____1618
John Earsden_____1618
John Maynard_____1611
Francis Pilkington_____1605
Walter Porter_____1632
Philip Rosseter_____1601

Contrasted with this long list, the number of those who seem to have even an indirect acquaintance with Catullus is very small indeed:

(1) In John Bartlet's *Book of Airs* (1606), the tenth song is an amplification of Gascoigne's *The Praise of Philip Sparrow* (1575) which was, of course, an elaboration of Catullus's "sparrow" poems, *Carm.* ii and iii:

> Of all the birds that I do know,
>   Philip my sparrow hath no peer;
> For sit she high, or sit she low,
>   Be she far off or be she near,
> There is no bird so fair, so fine,
> Nor yet so fresh as this of mine;
> For when she once hath felt a fit,
> Philip will cry still: yet, yet, yet.

So the poem goes on for four stanzas more; here, to be sure, we are very far from the original, but the thread of relation, though tenuous, is sufficiently discernible.

(2) From John Dowland's *A Pilgrim's Solace* (1612), the twentieth song:

> Hymen, O Hymen! mine
> Of treasures more divine
> What deity is like to thee
> That freest from mortality?

See *Carm.* lxi, 64-65, where like praise is given to Hymen:

> Quis huic deo
> Comparier ausit?

(3)   In Alfonso Ferrabosco's *Airs* (1609) Jonson's *Come, my Celia, let us prove* is included as *Air vi*. See my chapter on Jonson, quotation (1).

(4)   In the same song book, *Air ix*, we have the lines:
>   Turning all our sweetest nights
>   Into millions of delights,
>   And strive with many thousand kisses
>   To multiply exchange of blisses.

This may be a reference to the numbering of kisses in *Carm*. v.

(5)   From Robert Jones's *Ultimum Vale* (1608), the eighteenth air (repeated almost word for word in the twenty-first):
>   Thy words and oaths are light as wind,
>   And yet far lighter is thy mind.

Perhaps a reference to the often quoted *Carm*. lxx, 3-4.

(6)   From William Corkine's *Second Book of Airs* (1612), the eleventh song:
>   My dearest mistress, let us live and love,
>   And care not what old doting fools reprove.
>   Let us not fear their censure nor esteem
>   What they of us and of our loves shall deem.
>   Old Age's critic and censorious brow
>   Cannot of youthful dalliance allow,
>   Nor never could endure that we should taste
>   Of those delights which they themselves are past

This is clearly inspired by the opening lines of *Carm*. v, the *Vivamus, mea Lesbia*.

Campion, the greatest of the writers of song books, I have considered elsewhere, in the first chapter of this study, pp. 21-28.

BEN JONSON
(1573-1637)

The classical influence in Jonson's lyric poetry is of extreme importance; indeed, without his knowledge of the ancient writers Jonson would not have been Jonson: they stimulated his own poetic powers and formed the greater part of the material on which those powers were to work. He is the "first of our classical poets."[1] Many of his poems are drawn, almost in detail, from the Greek and Latin poets. On the whole, Jonson used his borrowings with great skill, Swinburne to the contrary, who maintains that "a worse translator than Ben Jonson never committed a double outrage on two languages at once."[2] His contemporaries admired greatly and praised greatly Jonson's painstaking devotion to the classics and his devotion to classical form. Carew bids him

> Repine not at the taper's thrifty waste
> That sleeks thy terser poems;[3]

and Randolph acclaims him as closely allied to the great ancient poets:

> I am akin to heroes, being thine,
> And part of my alliance is divine,
> Orpheus, Musaeus, Homer too, beside
> Thy brothers by the Roman mother's side,
> As Ovid, Virgil, and the Latin lyre
> That is so like thee, Horace. . . .[4]

Modern critics are not agreed as to the merits of Jonson's imitations of the classic authors; Professor Grierson denies to him "the ease and urbanity of Horace," but declares that he has, at his best, the "classical relevancy and restraint."[5] Swinburne's opinion we have had; M. Castelain levels against his lyric poetry a damning charge indeed: "L'ennui avec Jonson, c'est qu'on ne sait jamais, en l'admirant, si l'on n'est pas la dupe d'une fraude innocente ou plutôt de sa propre ignorance. . . . Qui nous dit que certains vers charmants ne viennent pas en droit ligne de Catulle ou d'Anacréon? que tel passage admiré par nous n'est pas une simple traduction bien faite ou une ingénieuse adaptation?"[6] Another critic is more kind, and, I think, more just in saying that Jonson "adapts to his needs, partly in compliment, pieces of the Latin fabric which he would preserve for English use. Or it may be that a lively memory is the prompter, unconsciously, of the theft."[7] Here again, as with M. Castelain, Catullus is the ancient source which the critic has foremost in mind.

What, specifically, is the Catullian influence in Jonson? First of all, it is, comparatively, much less pronounced than that of several other Latin poets. In his valuable treatise on the Latin element in Jonson's non-dramatic poetry Professor

---

1 Grierson, *The Literature of the First Half of the Seventeenth Century*, p. 153.
2 Swinburne, *A Study of Ben Jonson*, p. 111.
3 Carew, *To Ben Jonson* (Muses Library Edition, p. 91).
4 Randolph, *A Gratulatory to Ben Jonson* (Hazlitt's edition, p. 537).
5 Grierson, *op. cit.*, p. 161.
6 Castelain, *Ben Jonson, L' Homme et L'Oeuvre*, p. 838.
7 G. Gregory Smith, *Ben Jonson*, p. 225.

Malcolm Wilder has shown that Jonson's principal sources are Martial, Ovid, and Horace.[8] Catullus, in Professor Wilder's reckoning, makes a poor fourth. I have added somewhat, I think, to his list of instances of Catullian influence, but the supremacy of Martial and Horace remains unimpugned. Yet, as we shall see, the Catullian element is far from inconsiderable.

(1) From *The Forest*, Number V, *To Celia* (Gifford and Cunningham, *Works*, VIII, p. 255). This poem is also found in *Volpone*, III, v.

> Come, my Celia, let us prove,
> While we may, the sports of love;
> Time will not be ours for ever:
> He at length our good will sever.
> Spend not then his gifts in vain.
> *Suns that set may rise again;*
> *But if once we lose this light,*
> *'Tis with us perpetual night.*
> Why should we defer our joys?
> Fame and rumour are but toys.
> Cannot we delude the eyes
> Of a few poor household spies;
> Or his easier ears beguile,
> So removed by our wile?
> 'Tis no sin love's fruit to steal,
> But the sweet theft to reveal:
> 'Tis to be taken, to be seen,
> These have crimes accounted been.

The entire poem is unquestionably Catullian in inspiration and manner, but only in the three italicized lines has Jonson drawn directly upon the Latin poet. See *Carm.* v, 4-6:

> Soles occidere et redire possunt;
> Nobis, cum semel occidit brevis lux,
> Nox est perpetua una dormienda.

(2) From *The Forest*, Number VI, *To The Same* (G. and C., VIII, p. 255)

> Kiss me, sweet: the wary lover
> Can your favors keep, and cover,
> When the common courting jay
> All your bounties will betray.
> Kiss again: no creature comes.
> Kiss and score up wealthy sums
> On my lips thus hardly sundred,
> While you breathe. First give a hundred,
> Then a thousand, then another
> Hundred, then unto the other

---

8   M. L. Wilder, *Jonson's Indebtedness to Latin Authors, Shown Chiefly In His Non-Dramatic Poems*, pp. 244 ff.

Add a thousand, and so more:
Till you equal with the store,
All the grass that Rumney yields,
Or the sands in Chelsea fields,
Or the drops in silver Thames,
Or the stars that gild his streams,
In the silent Summer-nights
When youths ply their stolen delights;
That the curious may not know
How to tell 'em as they flow,
And the envious, when they find
What their number is, be pined.

For lines 6-11, cf. *Carm.* v, 7-9:

Da mi basia mille, deinde centum,
Dein mille altera, dein secunda centum,
Deinde usque altera mille, deinde centum.

Lines 12-20 are a paraphrase and adaptation of *Carm.* vii, 3-12:

Quam magnus numerus Libyssae harenae
Laserpiciferis iacet Cyrenis,
Oraclum Iovis inter aestuosi
Et Batti veteris sacrum sepulcrum,
Aut quam sidera multa, cum tacet nox,
Furtivos hominum vident amores,
Tam te basia multa basiare
Vesano satis et super Catullo est,
Quae nec pernumerare curiosi
Possint nec mala fascinare lingua.

The concluding two lines are drawn from *Carm.* v, 12-13:

Aut ne quis malus invidere possit,
Cum tantum sciat esse basiorum.

M. Castelain declares that these songs "ne sont qu'une libre traduction du *Vivamus, mea Lesbia* de Catulle," and asks "puisqu'il n'a pas su le faire oublier, à qui revient tout le mérite du morceau, sinon au poète latin?"[9] He is utterly mistaken in taking the two poems together in this way; the first poem is anything but a servile imitation; it is rather, in Mr. Smith's excellent phrase, an "open challenge to Catullus in one of his best known passages."[10] The second poem is, indeed, almost a composite of passages from Catullus, but there is much ingenuity in adaptation and grace in arrangement; it is surely, as Gifford well insists, not a translation.[11] The concluding four lines of the second song are found again in *Volpone*, III, v.

(3) From the *Forest*, XII, *Epistle to Elizabeth, Countess of Rutland* (G. and C., VIII, p. 269):

---

9 Castelain, *op. cit.*, p. 838.
10 Smith, *op. cit.*, p. 225.
11 Gifford and Cunningham, *Works of Ben Jonson*, VIII, p. 256.

Who made a lamp of Berenice's hair,
Or lifted Cassiopeia in her chair,
But only poets, rapt with rage divine?
The first line is clearly an echo of *Carm.* lxvi, *passim*.

(4)   From *The Underwoods*, XLVI, *An Ode* (G. and C., VIII, p. 375):
Was Lesbia sung by learn'd Catullus,
Or Delia's graces by Tibullus?
Doth Cynthia, in Propertius' song,
Shine more than she the stars among?
The reference is, of course, to the Lesbia poems, *Carmina*, *passim*.

(5) From *The Underwoods*, LVIII, *An Elegy* (G. and C., VIII, p. 391):
Or think you heaven is deaf, or hath no eyes?
Or those it hath, wink at your perjuries?
See, for a rather close parallel, *Carm.* xxx, 3-4, 11-12:
Iam me prodere, iam non dubitas fallere, perfide?
Num facta impia fallacum hominum caelicolis placent?. . .
Si tu oblitus es, at di meminerunt, meminit Fides,
Quae te ut paeniteat postmodo facti faciet tui.

(6)   *Ibid.*:
Are vows so cheap with women? or the matter
Whereof they are made, that they are writ in water,
And blown away with wind?
See *Carm.* lxx, 3-4:
Dicit: sed mulier cupido quod dicit amanti
In vento et rapida scribere opportet aqua.

(7)   *Ibid.*:
—When he dies
May wolves tear out his heart, vultures his eyes,
Swine eat his bowels, and his falser tongue
That uttered all, be to some raven flung;
And let his carrion corse be a longer feast
To the King's dogs, than any other beast!
These lines, utterly unnoticed by any editor, seem clearly to have been inspired by
Carm. cviii, 3-6:
Non equidem dubito quin primum inimica bonorum
Lingua exsecta avido sit data vulturio,
Effossos oculos voret atro gutture corvus,
Intestina canes, cetera membra lupi.

(8)   From *Underwoods*, LIX, *An Elegy* (G. and C., VIII, p. 393):
That love's a bitter sweet I ne'er conceive,
Till the sour minute comes of taking leave.
For the first line, see *Carm.* lxviii, 17-18:
Non est dea nescia nostri
Quae dulcem curis miscet amaritiem.

(9)   From *Underwoods*, LXI, *An Execration upon Vulcan* (G. and C., VIII, p. 399):

>   And why to me thus, thou lame Lord of Fire!
>   What had I done that might call on thine ire?

For "lame lord" see *Carm.* xxxvi, 7-8:

>   Scripta tardipedi deo daturam
>   Infelicibus ustilanda lignis.

(10)   *Underwoods*, XCIII, *Epithalamion on the Nuptials of Mr. Hierome Weston* (G.and C., IX, p. 23) is plainly modeled, in large part, upon *Carm.* lxi, and shot through with stray phrases reminiscent of Catullus's great epithalamion. We have not, indeed, anything to correspond to the long invocation to Hymen, but the various parts of Jonson's poem—the description of the bridal party and procession, the praise of the bride and bridegroom, the predictions of supreme marital delight, and the concluding hopes for the married couple's propagating a sturdy race—all follow the Catullian formula. The poem is too long, and, indeed, too full of matter having no bearing on our subject at all, to be quoted in full, but the following examples may suffice:

(a)   See how she paceth forth in virgin-white. . .

See *Carm.* lxi, 76-77:

>   Claustra pandite ianuae,
>   Virgo adest. . . .

(b)   Stay, thou wilt see what rites the virgins do,
>   The choicest virgin-troop in all the land!

See *Carm.* lxi, 36-38:

>   Vosque item simul, integrae
>   Virgines, quibus advenit
>   Par dies, agite in modum. . . .

(c)   — Such a race,
>   We pray may grace
>   Your fruitful spreading vine,
>   But dare not ask our wish in language Fescennine.

See *Carm.* lxi, 212-215:

>   Non decet
>   Tam vetus sine liberis
>   Nomen esse, sed indidem
>   Semper ingenerari.

and *Carm.* lxi, 126-7:

>   Ne diu taceat procax
>   Fescennina iocatio.

(d)   With chaste desires,
>   The holy perfumes of the marriage-bed,
>   Be kept alive, those sweet and sacred fires
>   Of love between you and your lovely-head!

That when you both are old,
    You find no cold
There, but renewed, say,
    After the last child born, This is our wedding-day.

See *Carm.* lxi, 156-163:

En tibi domus ut potens
Et beata viri tui
Quae tibi sine serviat. . . .
Usque dum tremulum movens
Cana tempus anilitas
Omnia omnibus annuit.

(e) Till you behold a race to fill your hall,
    A Richard and a Hierome. . . .
    And 'tween their grandsires' thighs
        Like pretty spies
    Peep forth a gem. . . .

See *Carm.* lxi, 216-218:

Torquatus volo parvulus
Matris a gremio suae
Porrigens teneras manus. . . .

(f) They both are slipp'd to bed; shut fast the door,
    And let him freely gather love's first fruits. . . .

See *Carm.* lxi, 231-235:

Claudite ostia, virgines:
Lusimus satis. At, boni
Coniuges, bene vivite et
Munere adsiduo valentem
Exercete iuventam.

(11) From the *Epigrams*, XLIX, *To Playwright* (G. and C., VIII, p. 169):
Playwright me reads, and still my verses damns,
He says I want the tongue of epigrams;
I have no salt, no bawdry he doth mean;
For witty, in his language, is obscene. . . .

See *Carm.* xvi, 6-9:

Versiculos. . . .
Qui tum denique habent salem ac leporem,
Si sunt molliculi ac parum pudici
Et quod pruriat incitare possunt.

(12) From the *Epigrams*, LXI, *To Fool, or Knave* (G. and C., VIII, 176):
Thy praise or dispraise is to me alike,
One does not stroke me, nor the other strike.

For a parallel epigram, see *Carm.* xciii:

Nil nimium studeo, Caesar, tibi velle placere,
    Nil scire utrum sis albus an ater homo.

Turning now to the consideration of lyrical passages in Jonson's semi-dramatic works, the masques, we find that he is very much indebted to the *Epithalamia* of Catullus.

(13)   From the *Masque of Hymen* (G. and C., VII, p. 61):
> O Juno, Hymen, Hymen, Juno! who
>   Can merit with you two?
> Without your presence, Venus can do nought
>   Save what with shame is bought;
> No father can himself a parent show,
>   Nor any house with prosperous issue grow.
> O then, what deities will dare
>   With Hymen or with Juno to compare?

See *Carm.* lxi, 61-63, 66-70:
> Nil potest sine te Venus
> Fama quod bona comprobet
> Commodi capere. . . .
> Nulla quit sine te domus
> Liberos dare, nec parens
> Stirpe nitier; at potest
> Te volente. Quis huic deo
> Comparier ausit?

(14)   *Ibid.* (G. and C., VII, p. 64):
> Up, youths! hold up your lights in air,
> And shake abroad their flaming hair.

See *Carm.* lxi, 77-78:
> Viden ut faces
> Splendidas quatiunt comas.

(15)   The Epithalamion in the *Masque of Hymen* (G. and C., VII, pp. 65-69) is full of allusions to Catullus.

(a)   Shrink not, soft virgin, you will love,
> Anon, what you so fear to prove.

See *Carm.* lxi, 94-95:
> Sed moraris, abit dies:
> Prodeas, nova nupta.

(b)   For the continually recurring chorus:
> On Hymen, Hymen call
> This night is Hymen's all,

see *Carm.* lxi, 123-124:
> Ite, concinite in modum
> 'O Hymen, Hymenaee io. . .'

(c)   Help, youths and virgins, help to sing
> The prize, which Hymen here doth bring.
>   And did so lately rap
>   From forth the mother's lap,

To place her by that side
Where she must long abide.

See *Carm.* lxi, 56-59:

Tu fero iuveni in manus
Floridam ipse puellulam
Dedis a gremio suae
Matris. . . .

(d) See! Hesperus is still in view.
What star can so deserve of you?

See *Carm.* lxii, 1-2:

Vesper Olympo
Exspectata diu vix tandem lumina tollit.

(e) Your bride, that, ere the morn,
Shall far more perfect be,
And rise as bright as he [i. e., *Hesperus*];
When like to him her name
Is changed, but not her fame.

See *Carm.* lxiv, 376-377 (a possible, but somewhat uncertain, reference):

Non illam nutrix orienti luce revisens
Hesterno collum poterit circumdare filo.

See also *Carm.* lxii, 35:

Hespere, mutato comprendis nomine eosdem.

(f) Haste your own good to meet;
And lift your golden feet
Above the threshold high,
With prosperous augury.

See *Carm.* lxi, 166-168:

Transfer omine cum bono
Limen aureolos pedes,
Rasilemque subi forem.

(g) Now, youths, let go your pretty arms.

See *Carm.* lxi, 181-182:

Mitte bracchiolum teres,
Praetextate, puellulae.

(h) Good matrons, that so well are known
To aged husbands of your own,
Place you our bride tonight,
And snatch away the light.

See *Carm.* lxi, 186-188:

O bonae senibus viris
Cognitae bene feminae,
Conlocate puellulam.

(i) So! now you may admit him in;
The act he covets is no sin,
But chaste and holy love,
Which Hymen doth approve;

> Without whose hallowing fires
> All aims are base desires.

See *Carm.* lxi, 191:

> Iam licet venias, marite;

and lxi, 61-63, quoted in (13).

> (j) Let ivy not so bind
> As when your arms are twined.

See *Carm.* lxi, 106-109:

> Lenta quin velut adsitas
> Vitis implicat arbores,
> Implicabitur in tuum
> Complexum.

> (k) And Venus, thou, with timely seed,
> Which may their after-comforts breed,
> Inform the gentle womb;
> Nor let it prove a tomb:
> But, ere ten months be wasted,
> The birth, by Cynthia hasted.

See *Carm.* lxi, 211-212:

> Ludite ut libet, et brevi
> Liberos date.

> (l) And when the babe to light is shown,
> Let it be like each parent known;
> Much of the father's face,
> More of the mother's grace;
> And either grandsire's spirit,
> And fame let it inherit.

See *Carm.* lxi, 221-225:

> Sit suo similis patri
> Manlio et facile insciis
> Noscitetur ab omnibus
> Et pudicitiam suae
> Matris indicet ore.

> (m) Cease, youths and virgins, you have done;
> Shut fast the door.

See *Carm.* lxi, 231-232:

> Claudite ostia, virgines:
> Lusimus satis.

> (16) From *The Barriers*, (G. and C., VII, pp. 78-79):
> Look, how a flower that close in closes grows,
> Hid from rude cattle, bruised with no ploughs,
> Which th'air doth stroke, sun strengthen, showers shoot higher,
> It many youths, and many maids desire;
> The same, when cropt by cruel hand 'tis wither'd,
> No youths at all, no maidens have desired:

> So a virgin, while untouch'd she doth remain,
> Is dear to hers; but when with body's stain
> Her chaster flower is lost, she leaves to appear
> Or sweet to young men, or to maidens dear.

This is a not too happy translation of *Carm.* lxii, 39-47:

> Ut flos in saeptis secretus nascitur hortis,
> Ignotus pecori, nullo convulsus aratro,
> Quem mulcent aurae, firmat sol, educat imber,
> Multi illum pueri, multae optavere puellae;
> Idem cum tenui carptus defloruit ungui,
> Nulli illum pueri, nullae optavere puellae:
> Sic virgo, dum intacta manet, dum cara suis est;
> Cum castum amisit polluto corpore florem,
> Nec pueris iucunda manet nec cara puellis.

(17)   From *The Barriers* (G. and C., VII, p. 80):

> ——As a lone vine, in a naked field,
> Never extols her branches, never bears
> Ripe grapes, but with a headlong heaviness wears
> Her tender body, and her highest sprout
> Is quickly leveled with her fading root;
> By whom no husbandman, no youths will dwell;
> But if, by fortune, she be married well
> To the elm her husband, many husbandmen
> And many youths inhabit by her, then:
> So whilst a virgin doth untouch'd abide,
> All unmanur'd, she grows old with her pride;
> But when to equal wedlock, in fit time,
> Her fortune and endeavor lets her climb,
> Dear to her love, and parents she is held.

This, the reply of Truth to the preceding speech of Opinion, translates the reply of the youths to the maidens, *Carm.* lxii, 49-58:

> Ut vidua in nudo vitis quae nascitur arvo
> Nunquam se extollit, nunquam mitem educat uvam,
> Sed tenerum prono deflectens pondere corpus
> Iam iam contingit summum radice flagellum,
> Hanc nulli agricolae, nulli accoluere iuvenci;
> At si forte eadem est ulmo coniuncta marito,
> Multi illam agricolae, multi accoluere iuvenci;
> Sic virgo dum intacta manet, dum inculta senescit;
> Cum par conubium maturo tempore adepta est,
> Cara viro magis et minus est invisa parenti.

(18) The Epithalamion in *The Hue and Cry after Cupid* (G. and C., VII, pp. 100-102) shows, in its form and spirit, traces of the influence upon Jonson of Catul-

lus's epithalamia, but the direct verbal borrowing is slight, as the poem is full of purely Jacobean conceits and extravagances.

(a) Up, youths and virgins, up and praise
     The god, whose nights outshine his days. . .

See *Carm.* lxi, 36-40, *et passim.*

(b) Shine, Hesperus, shine forth, thou wished star!

For this line, repeated again and again as a refrain, cf. *Carm.* lxii, 1-2.

(c)   Love's wealthy crop of kisses,
     And fruitful harvest of his mother's blisses. . .

See *Carm.* xlviii, 5-6:

> Non si densior aridis aristis
> Sit nostrae seges osculationis.

(d) That, ere the rosy-fingered morn
     Behold nine moons, there may be born
         A babe, t' uphold the fame
     Of Ratcliffe's blood and Ramsey's name, etc.

See *Carm.* lxi, 211-230.

(19)   From *The Masque of Queens* (G. and C., VII, p 134):
       Chaste Artemisia, the Carian dame,
       And fair-haired Beronice, Aegypt's fame.

Jonson, in his accompanying note, refers specifically to Catullus's *Coma Berenices, Carm.* lxvi.

Such, then, was the influence of Catullus in Jonson's lyrical verse; for completeness, I include certain instances of the Latin poet's influence drawn from Jonson's dramatic poetry or prose.

(20)   From *The Masque of Hymen* (G. and C., VII, p. 47), a stage-direction:
       On the other hand, entered Hymen (the god of marriage) in a saffron-colour'd robe, his under-vestments white, his socks yellow, a yellow veil of silk on his left arm, his head crowned with roses and marjoram, in his right hand a torch of pine tree.

See *Carm.* lxi, 6-10 and 14-15:

> Cinge tempora floribus
> Suave olentis amaraci,
> Flammeum cape, laetus huc,
> Huc veni niveo gerens
> Luteum pede soccum.
> . . . . Manu
> Pineam quate taedam.

(21)   From *The Poetaster*, III, i. (G. and C., II, p. 438):
       Hang him, fusty satyr, he smells all goat, he carries a ram under his arm holes, the slave.

See *Carm.* lxxi, 1:

> Si cui iure bono sacer alarum obstitit hircus.

(22)   From *Cynthia's Revels*, V, ii. (G. and C., III, p. 325):
> Taste, smell, I assure you, sir, pure benjamin, the only spirited scent
> that ever awaked a Neapolitan nostril. You would wish yourself all nose
> for the love on't.

See *Carm.* xiii, 13-14:
> Quod tu cum olfacies, deos rogabis
> Totum ut te faciant, Fabulle, nasum.

(23)   From *The Alchemist*, I, i. (G. and C., III, p. 13):
> At Pie Corner. . . .
> Where, like the father of hunger, you did walk
> Piteously costive.

See *Carm.* xxi, 1:
> Aureli, pater esuritionum.

(24)   The motto for *A Tale of a Tub:*
> Infaceto est infacetior rure.

See *Carm.* xxii, 14.

Harrington suggests that *Drink to me only with thine eyes* (G. and C., VIII, p. 258) may have been suggested by Catullus, and instances *Carmina* lxx and lxii.[12] There are two lines, indeed, reminiscent of Catullus:
> But might I of Jove's nectar sup
> I would not change for thine,

for which likeness see *Carm.* lxx, 1-2:
> Nulli se dicit mulier mea nubere malle
>   Quam mihi, non si se Iuppiter ipse petat,

and *Carm.* lxxii, 1-2:
> Dicebas quondam solum te nosse Catullum,
>   Lesbia, nec prae me velle tenere Iovem.

Neither of the passages, however, is very closely akin to Jonson's lines, and it has long since been pointed out that Jonson's real source for this poem was the Greek sophist Philostratus.[13]

Esther Cloudman Dunn quotes from Jonson's *Epicoene*, I. i. (G. and C., I, p. 407):
> Give me a look, give me a face,
> That makes simplicity a grace:
> Robes loosely flowing, hair as free;
> Such sweet neglect more taketh me,
> Then all the adulteries of art;
> They strike mine eyes; but not my heart,

---

12   Harrington, *op. cit.*, pp. 164-165.
13   Gifford and Cunningham, VIII, 259-260, n.

and goes on to say that "Jonson here finds opportunity for one more echo of a pretty idea which runs from Catullus to Herrick."[14] I have been able to find nothing of the sort in Catullus, though, to be sure, it is the theme of one of Herrick's best-known lyrics. As a matter of fact, this lyric, as Moorman, among others, points out, is "based upon a Latin poem by the sixteenth-century French poet, Jean Bonnefons."[15]

---

14   Esther Cloudman Dunn, *Ben Jonson's Art*, p. 70.
15   F. W. Moorman, *Robert Herrick: A Critical and Biographical Study*, pp. 190-191.

THOMAS RANDOLPH
(1605-1635)

The traces of Catullus in Randolph are comparatively few. With him hot passions and a certain lusty joy in living were the sources of most of his verse; the part which the ancients played in furnishing material for his poems was comparatively small. He was, however, like Cartwright, a "son of Ben," and he had an elegan⁺, if superficial, knowledge of the erotic poets of Rome. Strangely enough, in quotation (4) of this chapter we have a most recondite reference to one of the less known parts of one of the more unfamiliar *Carmina*, which would seem to indicate that Randolph knew his Catullus at first hand (though, indeed, his mere association with Jonson might well bring him knowledge of such a passage), and not merely by references which he might have chanced upon in many of his fellow poets. A reference to the *Vivamus, mea Lesbia* proves not at all conclusively that a poet knew Catullus, so often is that poem met with in the seventeenth century in translation and paraphrase; a reference to such a passage as our (4) is conclusive as to some actual knowledge of the Latin poet.

(1)   From the *Complaint to Venus:*
      And see how I shall touch my powerful lyre,
      And more inspir'd with thine than Phoebus' fire
      Chant such a moving verse as shall soon frame
      Desire of dalliance in the coyest dame,
      Melting to amorous thoughts her heart of stone,
      And force her to untruss her virgin zone.

Perhaps an echo of the function Catullus assigns to the poet of love, *Carm.* xvi, 6-9:

      . . . .Versiculos. . . .
      Qui tum denique habent salem ac leporem,
      Si sunt molliculi ac parum pudici,
      Et quod pruriat incitare possunt. . . .

(2)   From *An Epithalamium:*
      Maids, dance as nimbly as your blood,
      Which I see swell a purple flood,
      In emulation of that good

      The bride possesseth; for I deem
      What she enjoys will be the theme
      This night of every virgin's dream.

      See how the lusty bridegroom's veins
      Swell, till the active torrent strains
      To break those o'er stretch'd azure chains.

And the fair bride, ready to cry
To see her pleasant loss so nigh,
Pants like the sealed pigeon's eye. . .

And in such strict embraces twine
The ivy and the columbine. . . .

Thence may there spring many a pair
Of sons and daughters, strong and fair;
How soon the gods have heard my prayer!

Methinks already I espy
The cradles rock, the babies cry,
And drowsy nurses' lullaby.

The likeness, in manner, choice of incident, and even in phrase (cf. "And in such close embraces twine," etc. with *Carm.* lxi, 106-109), of this exquisite poem to the sixty-first carmen of Catullus is, to my mind, marked; the influence of the Latin poet is, however, too pervasive and, so, too indefinable to warrant lengthy quotation. See *Carm.* lxi, *passim.*

(3)   From *An Epithalamium to Mr. F. H.:*
        . . . Let their affections meet
      Witn happy omens in the genial sheet.
Perhaps an echo of *Carm.* lxi, 166-167:
      Transfer omine cum bono
      Limen aureolos pedes.

(4)   From *An Eclogue to Master Jonson:*
      The thirsty pilgrim travelling by land,
      When the fierce Dog-star doth the day command,
      Half choked with dust, parched with the sultry heat,
      Tir'd with the journey, and o'ercome with sweat,
      Finding a gentle spring, at her cool brink
      Doth not with more delight sit down and drink,
      Than I record his songs.
This is clearly inspired by *Carm.* lxviii, 57-62
      Qualis in aerii perlucens vertice montis
          Rivus muscoso prosilit e lapide,
      Qui, cum de prona praeceps est valle volutus,
          Per medium densi transit iter populi,
      Dulce viatori lasso in sudore levamen
          Cum gravis exustos aestus hiulcat agros.

(5)   From *A Pastoral Courtship:*
      Come, let those thighs, those legs, those feet
      With mine in thousand windings meet,
      Woven into more subtle vines
      Than woodbine ivy, or the vines.
See *Carm.* lxi, 106-109, already several times quoted.

(6)　*Ibid.:*

Now let us kiss. Would you be gone?
Manners at least allow me one.
Blush you at this? pretty one, stay,
And I will take that kiss away,
Thus, with a second, and that too
A third wipes off; so will we go
To numbers that the stars outrun,
And all the atoms in the sun.

For this reckoning of kisses see *Carm.* v, already quoted, and for the comparison of the kisses to the numbers of the stars, see *Carm.* vii, 7.

(7)　*Ibid.:*

View all the fields, survey the bowers,
The buds, the blossoms, and the flowers,
And say if they so rich could be
In barren poor virginity.

See, for a possible source, the comparison to a maiden of a barren vine, *Carm.* lxii, 49-58.

We have in Randolph's poems two mentions of a Lesbia: one Lesbia is a woman of gallantry who has a kept youth for her purposes (see *In Lesbiam et Histrionem*):

I wonder what should Madam Lesbia mean
To keep young Histrio, and for what scene
So bravely she maintains him, that what sense
He please to bless, 'tis done at her expense!

This may be a reference to Catullus's unprincipled mistress; in the other poem, *Upon a very Deformed Gentlewoman, with a Voice incomparably sweet,* a Lesbia is the unfortunate lady in question; here I can see no relation to Catullus's mistress.

THOMAS CAREW
(1594-1639)

Carew was deeply influenced by both Jonson and Donne—he had the careful
devotion to form and the interest in graceful allusion of the first, and the tendency
toward subtlety and realism which distinguished the second. We have seen, in the
chapters on Jonson and Donne, how he could felicitate Jonson on

> The taper's thrifty waste

> That sleeks thy terser poems,[1]

that is, on his studious devotion to the classics; and, again, apostrophize the dead
Donne for having driven the classical tradition out of English poetry.[2] Perhaps,
after all, he inclined rather more to the school of Jonson than to that of Donne;
he was, at any rate, thoroughly classical in his devotion to form and to careful
elaboration. For this characteristic of his, to be sure, Suckling ridiculed him in a
barbed stanza:

> Tom Carew was next, but he had a fault,

> That would not well stand with a laureat;

> His muse was hide-bound, and th' issue of's brain

> Was seldom brought forth but with trouble and pain.[3]

But Carew's classicism is one of his most valuable attributes; Professor Schelling
says admirably of Carew and Herrick: "These poets are English, like their masters
Jonson and Donne, and entirely free from Italianism. Their classicism sits easily
upon them, especially that of Carew, and is the classicism of men of the world,
informing their style and illuminating their thoughts, not encumbering them with
unnecessary learning."[4] Legouis in like manner attributes to him the "logical good
order of the classicists."[5] Carew, as will be seen from the quotations that follow,
knew Catullus, but he uses his knowledge sparingly; the references are never
patently taken from the Latin; with great skill and delicacy of taste he moulds to
his own use what he borrows. Once more to make use of Professor Schelling's
happy words, Catullus, like classicism, "sits easily upon him."

(1)   From *Secrecy Protested* (Vincent, p. 13):

> No ear shall hear our love, but we

> Silent as the night will be.

> The God of love himself. . . .

> Shall never know that we can tell

> What sweets in stolen embraces dwell.

See *Carm.* vii, 7-8:

> . . . Quam sidera multa, cum tacet nox,

> Furtivos hominum vident amores,

---

1 See p. 49.
2 See p. 37.
3 Suckling, *A Session of the Poets* (Thompson's edition, p. 10).
4 Schelling, *A Book of Seventeenth Century Lyrics*, p. xxxv.
5 Emile Legouis, *A History of English Literature, 650-1660*, p. 347.

and *Carm.* lxviii, 145:

> Sed furtiva dedit mira munuscula nocte.

(2) From *Conquest by Flight* (Vincent, p. 19):
> Ladies, fly from love's smooth tale,
> Oaths steep'd in tears do oft prevail;
>
> . . . .
>
> Then stop your ears, when lovers cry,
> Lest yourselves weep, when no soft eye
> Shall with a sorrowing tear repay
> The pity which you cast away.

See, for a possible influence, *Carm.* lxiv, 145-148:

> Quis dum aliquid cupiens animus praegestit apisci,
> Nil metuunt iurare, nihil promittere parcunt:
> Sed simul ac cupidae mentis satiata libido est,
> Dicta nihil meminere, nihil periuria curant.

(3) From *To an Inconstant Mistress* (Vincent, p. 20):
> When thou, poor excommunicate
>   From all the joys of love, shalt see
> The full reward and glorious fate
>   Which my strong faith shall purchase me,
>   Then curse thine own inconstancy.
>
> Then shalt thou weep, entreat, complain
>   To Love, as I did once to thee;
> When all thy tears shall be as vain
>   As mine were then, and thou shalt be
>   Damn'd for thy false apostasy.

This is reminiscent of Catullus's prediction concerning the future of *his* inconstant mistress, already quoted, *Carm.* viii, 12-19:

> Vale, puella! iam Catullus obdurat,
> Nec te requiret nec rogabit invitam;
> At tu dolebis, cum rogaberis nulla. . .

(4) From *To Her in Absence: a Ship* (Vincent, p. 30):
> Toss'd in a troubled sea of griefs, I float
> Far from the shore, in a storm-beaten boat.

See *Carm.* lxiv, 62:

> Prospicit et magnis curarum fluctuat undis,

and *Carm.* lxv, 4:

> . . . . Tantis fluctuat ipsa malis.

Vergil, to be sure, borrowed the phrase from Catullus and may be Carew's source; see *Aeneid*, VIII, 19:

> . . . . Magno curarum fluctuat aestu.

(5) From *To Ben Jonson* (Vincent, p. 91):
> Repine not at the taper's thrifty waste,
> That sleeks thy terser poems. . . .
> Let others glut on the extorted praise
> Of vulgar breath; trust thou to after days:
> Thy labour'd works shall live, when time devours
> Th' abortive offspring of their hasty hours.

See *Carm.* xcv:
> Zmyrna mei Cinnae nonam post denique messem
>   Quam coepta est nonamque edita post hiemem,
> Milia cum interea quingenta Hortensius uno.
>
> . . . .
>
> Zmyrna cavas Satrachi penitus mittetur ad undas,
>   Zmyrnam cana diu saecula pervolent.
> At Volusi annales Paduam morientur ad ipsam
>   Et laxas scombris saepe dabunt tunicas.
> Parva mei mihi sint cordi monumenta sodalis:
>   At populus tumido gaudeat Antimacho.

(6) From *On the Marriage of T. K. to C. C., the Morning Stormy* (Vincent, p. 112):
> Then boldly to the fight of love proceed!
> 'Tis mercy not to pity, though she bleed.
> We'll strew no nuts, but change that ancient form. . . .

For the last line, see *Carm.* lxi, 128:
> Nec nuces pueris neget.

There is a similar reference in Vergil; see *Eclogues*, VIII, 29.

(7) From *A New Year's Gift to the King* (Vincent, p. 124):
> Happy auspicious days appear,
> Mark'd with a whiter stone. . . .

See *Carm.* lxviii, 147-148:
> Quare illud satis est, si nobis is datur unis
>   Quem lapide illa diem candidiore notat.

(8) From *The Complement* (Vincent, p. 139):
> I love not for those eyes, nor hair,
> Nor cheeks, nor lips, nor teeth so rare,
> Nor for thy speech, thy neck, nor breast,
> Nor for thy belly, nor the rest,
> Nor for thy hand nor foot so small;
> But would'st thou know, dear sweet, for all.

Perhaps suggested by *Carm.* lxxxvi, 5-6:
> Lesbia formosa est, quae cum pulcherrima tota est,
>   Tum omnibus una omnis subripuit Veneres.

(9)   From *To his Mistress Retiring in Affection* (Vincent, p. 172):
> But if my constant love shall fail to move thee,
> Then know my reason hates thee, though I love thee.

See *Carm.* lxxxv:
> Odi et amo,

and *Carm.* lxxii, 7-8:
> Qui potis est? inquis. Quod amantem iniuria talis
>   Cogit amare magis, sed bene velle minus.

WILLIAM CARTWRIGHT
(1611-1643)

William Cartwright was one of the "sons" of Ben Jonson, and imitated assiduously his great master in his devotion to the classical poets. The influence of Catullus is decidedly marked in Cartwright's comparatively small body of verse; he uses the Latin poet, in the main, with sympathy and taste. His knowledge of Catullus seems to have been thorough and inclusive; his *Ariadne Deserted*, for example, shows that he was well acquainted with certain of the minor details of Catullus's epyllion, *Carm.* lxiv, his longest poem; the grace and fancy with which he has elaborated the story of the plight of Ariadne is deserving of special notice and commendation.

(1)   From *A Song of Dalliance* (Goffin, *Life and Poems of William Cartwright*, p. 35):

> Call us wicked wanton men;
> Do as turtles, kiss and groan.

Perhaps an echo of *Carm.* lxviii, 125-127:

> Nec tantum niveo gavisa est ulla columbo
>   Compar, quae multo dicitur improbius
> Oscula mordenti semper decerpere rostro. . .

(2)   From *Falsehood* (Goffin, p. 37):

> She [Venus], O she make thee true to all,
> Marry an army, and then fall
> Through scornful hatred and disdain.
>   But mayst thou be
>   Still false to me. . .

This resembles greatly, to my mind, Catullus's scornful objurgation of his mistress, xi, 17-21:

> Cum suis vivat valeatque moechis,
> Quos simul complexa tenet trecentos,
> Nullum amans vere, sed identidem omnium
>   Ilia rumpens.
> Nec meum respectet, ut ante, amorem.

(3)   From *To The Memory of a Ship-wracked Virgin* (Goffin, p. 44):

> Harken, O winds (if that ye yet have ears,
> Who were thus deaf unto my fair one's tears).

Cartwright, as is seen by (10), was thoroughly familiar with *Ariadne's Complaint;* this makes it the more probable that the preceding lines were inspired by *Carm.* lxiv, 164-166:

> Sed quid ego ignaris nequiquam conqueror auris,
> Exsternata malo, quae nullis sensibus auctae
> Nec missas audire queunt nec reddere voces?

(4) *Lesbia, on her Sparrow* (Goffin, p. 46):
      Tell me not of joy! there's none;
      Now my little sparrow's gone!
            He just as you
            Would toy and woo,
        He would chirp and flatter me,
      He would hang the wing awhile
      Till at length he saw me smile.
            Lord! How sullen he would be!

      He would catch a crumb, and then
      Sporting let it go again,
            He from my lip
            Would moisture sip,
        He would from my trencher feed,
      Then would hop, and then would run,
      And cry Philip when h' had done,
            O whose heart can choose but bleed?

      O how eager would he fight?
      And ne'er hurt though he did bite:
            No morn did pass
            But on my glass
        He would sit, and mark and do
      What I did, now ruffle all
      His feathers o'er, now let 'em fall
            And then straightway sleek 'em too.

      Whence may Cupid get his darts
      Feather'd now to pierce our hearts?
            A wound he may,
            Nor Love convey.
        Now this faithful bird is gone,
      O let mournful turtles join
      With loving red-breasts, and combine
            To sing dirges o'r his stone.

This is not a translation of *Carm*. iii; Cartwright takes his theme and title from
Catullus and weaves into his poem many of the ideas of *Carmina* ii and iii, but
embroiders on them to suit his own fancy. The last stanza is entirely his own, save
in its relation to the general Catullian theme. Cartwright represents Lesbia as
herself bewailing the death of her sparrow; Catullus himself expresses grief for the
sparrow's death. For verbal likenesses see *Carm*. iii:

      Passer mortuus est meae puellae,
      Passer, deliciae meae puellae. . .
      Nec sese a gremio illius movebat,
      Sed circumsiliens modo huc modo illuc
      Ad solam dominam usque pipiabat;

and ii, 1-10:

> Passer, deliciae meae puellae,
> Quicum ludere, quem in sinu tenere,
> Cui primum digitum dare adpetenti
> Et acris solet incitare morsus,
> Cum desiderio meo nitenti
> Carum nescio quid liber iocari,
> (Et solaciolum sui doloris,
> Credo, ut tum gravis adquiescat ardor),
> Tecum ludere sicut ipsa possem
> Et tristis animi levare curas!

(5) From *To Lydia Whom Men Observ'd to Make Too Much of Me* (Goffin, p. 64):

> Let tongues be free, speak what they will,
> Say our love's loud, but let's love still.
> I hate a secret stifled flame,
> Let yours and mine have voice and name.

Probably inspired by *Carm.* lv, 15-20:

> Dic nobis ubi sis futurus, ede
> Audacter, comitte, crede luci.
> Nunc te lacteolae tenent puellae?
> Si linguam clauso tenes in ore,
> Fructus proicies amoris omnes:
> Verbosa gaudet Venus loquella.

(6) From *In Memory of the Most Worthy Ben Jonson* (Goffin, p. 109):

> No need to make good count'nance ill, and use
> The plea of strict life for a looser Muse.

See *Carm.* xvi, 5-6:

> Nam castum esse decet pium poetam
> Ipsum, versiculos nihil necesse est.

This sentiment is found in other Latin poets: in Ovid's *Tristia*, II, 354, *Vita verecunda est, Musa iocosa mea*, for example, and Martial, I, iv, 8, *Lasciva est nobis pagina, vita proba*. But, after all, they are merely repeating Catullus's defense.

(7) From *An Epithalamium on The Marriage of Lady Mary to the Prince of Orange his Son* (Goffin, p. 125):

> But when her zone shall come to be unty'd,
>   And she be twice your bride. . . .
>   Then you will know what bliss
>   Angels both have, and miss;
> How souls may mix and take fresh growth
> In neither whole, and whole in both;
>   Pleasures, that none can know. . .

This may be a reflection of *Carm.* lxi, 116-119:

> Quae tuo veniunt ero,
> Quanta gaudia, quae vaga
> Nocte, quae medio die
>   Gaudeat!

(8) *Ibid.* (Goffin, p. 125):

> D' you see? or am I false? your tender vine,
>   Methinks, on every twine
> Tiaras, sceptres, crowns, spoils, trophies wears. . .
>   Which, hanging in their beauteous shapes,
>   Adorn her boughs like swelling grapes.

This likening of a bride to a grape-vine we have already noticed in Catullus; see *Carm.* lxii, 49-50.

(9) From *November, Or, Signal Dayes Observed in that Month in Relation to the Crown and Royal Family* (Goffin, p. 150):

> That to the honor of this early bride
>   (Like Thetis joyn'd to Peleus side)
> Some tender thing may fall; though none can be
>   So white, so tender, as is she.

See *Carm.* lxiv, *passim.*

(10) From *Ariadne Deserted by Theseus, as She Sits upon a Rock in the Island Naxos, thus Complains* (Goffin, pp. 59-62). The whole poem is obviously inspired by the episode of Ariadne in *Carm.* lxiv; I quote only the more significant parallels:

(a) Theseus! O Theseus hark! but yet in vain
>   Alas deserted I complain;
> It was some neighboring rock, more soft than he,
>   Whose hollow bowels pitied me.

See lxiv, 132-133:

> Sicine me patriis avectam, perfide, ab aris,
> Perfide, deserto liquisti in litore, Theseu?

and, in Cartwright's spirit, 154-155:

> Quaenam te genuit sola sub rupe leaena,
> Quod mare conceptum spumantibus exspuit undis?

(b) Till my eyes drank up his,
>   And his drank mine,
> I ne'er thought souls might kiss
>   And spirits join. . .
> But his fair visage made me find
>   Pleasures and fears,
>   Hopes, sighs, and tears. . .

Catullus gives a like description of Ariadne on Theseus's coming, *Carm.* lxiv, 86-88, 91-93:

> Hunc simul ac cupido conspexit lumine virgo
> Regia, quam suavis exspirans castus odores

Lectulus in molli complexu matris alebat. . .
Non prius ex illo flagrantia declinavit
Lumina quam cuncto concepit corpore flammam
Funditus atque imis exarsit tota medullis.

(c) Yet for revenge to Heaven I'll call
And breathe one curse before I fall. . .
Mayst thou forget to wing thy ships with white,
That the black sail may to the longing sight
Of thy gray father tell thy fate, and he
Bequeath the sea his name, falling like me.

See *Carm.* lxiv, 188-190, 199-201, 243-245:

"Non tamen ante mihi languescent lumina morte,
Nec prius a fesso secedent corpore sensus
Quam iustam a divis exposcam prodita multam. . .
Vos nolite pati nostrum vanescere luctum,
Sed quali solam Theseus me mente reliquit,
Tali mente, deae, funestet seque suosque". . .
Cum primum inflati conspexit lintea veli,
Praecipitem sese scopulorum e vertice iecit,
Amissum credens immiti Thesea fato.

(d) And yet, O Nymphs, below who sit,
In whose swift floods his vows were writ. . .

See *Carm.* lxx, 3-4, several times quoted.

(e) Yonder, yonder,
Comes my dear. . .
See Satyrs dance along,
In a confused throng,
Whiles horns' and pipes' rude noise
Do mad their lusty joys,. . .

The passage quoted and the lines which follow it are obviously inspired by Catullus's spirited description of the coming of Bacchus, *Carm.* lxiv, 251-264:

At parte ex alia florens volitabat Iacchus
Cum thiaso satyrorum et Nysigenis silenis.
Te quaerens, Ariadna, tuoque incensus amore. . .
Quae tum alacres passim lymphata mente furebant
Euhoe bacchantes, euhoe capita inflectentes. . .
Multis raucisonos efflabant cornua bombos
Barbaraque horribili stridebat tibia cantu.

(11) From Cartwright's play, *The Royal Slave*, V, vii. (Goffin, p. 164):
But thou, O Sun, may'st set, and then
In brightness rise next morn again;
He, when he shall once leave this light,
Will make and have eternal night.

See *Carm.* v, 4-6, already several times quoted.

(12)   From Cartwright's play *The Ordinary*, IV, v. (**Goffin,** p. 170):
> Fair, we know, maids do refuse
> To grant what they do come to lose;
> Intend a conquest, you that wed;
> They would be chastely ravished.

Perhaps an echo of *Carm.* lxii, 36-37:
> At libet innuptis ficto te carpere questu.
> Quid tum, si carpunt tacita quem mente **requirunt?**

(13)   *Ibid.*, IV, v. (Goffin, p. 171):
> O may her arms wax black and blue
> Only by hard encircling you:
> May she round about you twine
> Like the easy twisting vine.

For the familiar figure see *Carm.* lxi, 106-109:
> Lenta quin velut adsitas
> Vitis implicat arbores,
> Implicabitur in tuum
> Complexum.

SIR JOHN SUCKLING
(1609-1642)

There is, so far as I can discover, no trace of the influence of Catullus in all of Suckling's poetry. The two poets could not have been further apart in their way of regarding the chief subject of their poetry, love; Suckling's gay indifference and reckless cynicism have nothing in common with the deep and passionate earnestness of Catullus. The cynic and the gallant make up the true Suckling; his "obvious cynicism where affairs of the heart were concerned," says Thompson, "expresses itself at once in verse. 'Why so pale and wan, fond lover?' is a happy impromptu in which the natural Suckling declares himself without reserve. When he turns to hymn constant love. . . he is writing conventionally and uneasily."[1] Wendell grants him, and rightly, "a touch of Jonson's grace," but declares that it is "weakened by careless triviality";[2] he himself is free in admitting his contempt for the poet's art:

> Suckling next was call'd, but did not appear,
> But strait one whisper'd Apollo i' th' ear,
> That of all men living he cared not for't,
> He loved not the Muses as well as his sport;
> And prized black eyes, or a lucky hit
> At bowls, above all the trophies of wit.[3]

He was not a man of letters, or, indeed, a lettered man; his acquaintance with the classics seems not to have been great.

---

1 A. Hamilton Thompson, *Works of Sir John Suckling*, p. xiv.
2 Barrett Wendell, *The Temper of the Seventeenth Century in English Literature*, p. 140.
3 *Works of Sir John Suckling*, p. 11.

WILLIAM BROWNE OF TAVISTOCK
(1591-1643)

The interminably long pastoral poems of Browne are narrative in form but essentially lyrical in manner and substance. They are worthless as stories—no one on coming to the end of *Brittannia's Pastorals* has any clear remembrance of the sequence of poor Walla's haps and mishaps: indeed, I think we can be fairly sure that Browne himself would have been at a loss to find any logical coherence in his pastorals. But they are truly lyrical in manner—one long, low, dulcet piping, never reaching any high poetic pitch, and never, or very seldom, ceasing to be poetry and sinking into the mere tinkling of rhyming lines.

Browne was of the school of Spenser, and possessed of all that "fastidious culture"[1] which distinguished that group of poets. His verse shows ever his acquaintance, not only with many of the great classic poets, but with the poets of the continent. Rather frequent are the direct references to the classical authors, real and mythological, as his masters in song:

> O had I Virgil's verse, or Tully's tongue,
> Or raping numbers like the Thracian's song,
> I have a theme would make the rocks to dance.[2]

Again he gives a list of the great authors he admired and imitated: Maro, Naso, Ariosto, Petrarch, Tasso, Du Bartas, Marot, Ronsard, and Garnier[3]—Latin, Italian, and French, chosen with utter catholicity. Ovid is clearly Browne's favorite Latin poet, and his references to him have much of the devotion of a pupil for his master:

> Exiled Naso (from whose golden pen
> The Muses did distil delights for men).[4]

No direct reference to Catullus is made anywhere in Browne's poetry, but there is clear evidence that he was acquainted with the Latin poet. Browne uses his borrowings from Catullus with taste and discernment; especially worthy of note is the frequency with which the Catullian simile of the vine and the tree occurs. That it is directly from Catullus the ninth quotation proves conclusively, since it is well nigh a paraphrase of Catullus's words.

(1) From Book I, Song I of *Brittannia's Pastorals*, ll. 37 ff.:
> She, whose passion. . .
> Bent all her course to him-wards, let him know
> He was the elm whereby her vine did grow.

For this figure, very frequently used by Browne, see (9), where the original passage from *Carm.* lxii is quoted in full.

(2) *Ibid.*, l. 73 ff:
> Running the mountains, fields, by wat'ry springs,
> Filling each cave with woeful echoings;

1   Wendell, *op. cit.*, p. 134.
2   *Brittannia's Pastorals*, Book I, Song IV, ll. 225-227.
3   *Ibid.*, Book II, Song I, l. 935 ff.
4   *Ibid.*, Book I, Song IV, ll. 697-698.

Making in thousand places her complaint,
And uttering to the trees what her tears meant.
See the description of the deserted and distraught Ariadne, *Carm.* lxiv, 124-128:
Saepe illam perhibent ardenti corde furentem
Clarisonas imo fudisse e pectore voces,
Ac tum praeruptos tristem conscendere montes
Unde aciem in pelagi vastos protenderet aestus,
Tum tremuli salis adversas procurrere in undas.

(3)　*Ibid.,* ll. 115 ff.:
But what? or can I cancel or unbind
That which my heart hath seal'd and love hath sign'd?
Ah, no, grief doth deceive me more each hour;
"For, who so truly loves, hath not that power."
There may possibly be an echo here of *Carm.* lxxvi, 10, 13-14:
Quare cur tu te iam amplius excrucies?. . .
Difficile est longum subito deponere amorem;
Difficile est, verum hoc qua libet efficias.

(4)　*Ibid.,* ll. 169 ff.:
Then stay a while:　the beasts that haunt those springs,
Of whom I hear the fearful bellowings,
May do that deed (as moved by my cry),
Whereby my soul, as spotless ivory,
May turn from whence it came.
For a close parallel, considering the similar plight of the two deserted maidens,
see Ariadne's complaint, *Carm.* lxiv, 152-153:
Pro quo dilaceranda feris dabor alitibusque
Praeda, neque iniecta tumulabor mortua terra.

(5)　From Book I, Song II of *Brittannia's Pastorals,* ll. 581 ff.:
She'll tell you what you call Virginity,
Is fitly liken'd to a barren tree;
Which when the gard'ner on it pains bestows,
To graft an imp thereon, in time it grows
To such perfection that it yearly brings
As goodly fruit as any tree that springs.
See the passage quoted in (9).

(6)　From Book II, Song I, *Brittannia's Pastorals,* ll. 150 ff.:
What wretch inhuman, or what wilder blood,
Suck'd in a desert from a tiger's brood,
Could leave her so disconsolate?
See the complaint of the deserted Ariadne, *Carm.* lxiv, 154:
Quaenam te genuit sola sub rupe leaena,
and *Carm.* lx, 1, 3:
Num te leaena montibus Libystinis. . . . .
Tam mente dura procreavit ac taetra. . .

(7)　From Book II, Song III, *Britannia's Pastorals*, ll. 1155 ff.:
I that have ever held all women be
Void of all worth if wanting chastity;
And whoso any lets that best flower pull
She might be fair, but never beautiful.
See *Carm.* lxii, 39-47:
Ut flos in saeptis secretus nascitur hortis. . .
——Cum tenui carptus defloruit ungui.
Nulli illum pueri, nullae optavere puellae.
Sic virgo dum intacta manet, dum cara suis est;
Cum castum amisit polluto corpore florem,
Nec pueris iucunda manet nec cara puellis.

(8)　From Book II, Song IV, *Britannia's Pastorals*, ll. 649 ff.:
　　　Then the light. . . .
Bewray'd an elm embraced by a vine
Clipping so strictly that they seem'd to be
One in their growth, one shade, one fruit, one tree.
For the passage from which this is imitated, see (9).

(9)　From Book II, Song V, *Britannia's Pastorals*, ll. 319 ff.:
For as with hanging head I have beheld
A widow vine stand in a naked field,
Unhusbanded, neglected, all forlorn,
Brows'd on by deer, by cattle cropp'd and torn,
Unpropp'd, unsuccoured by stake or tree
From wreakful storms' impetuous tyranny,
When, had a willing hand lent kind redress,
Her pregnant bunches might from out the press
Have sent a liquor both for taste and show
No less divine than those of Malligo:
Such was this wight, and such she might have been.
For this most frequent figure with Browne, already noticed in (1), (5), and (8)
above, see the almost identical passage in *Carm.* lxii, 49-56:
Ut vidua in nudo vitis quae nascitur arvo
Nunquam se extollit, nunquam mitem educat uvam. . .
Sed tenerum prono deflectens pondere corpus
Iam iam contingit summum radice flagellum,
Hanc nulli agricolae, nulli accoluere iuvenci;
At si forte eadem est ulmo coniuncta marito,
Multi illam agricolae, multi accoluere iuvenci:
Sic virgo, dum intacta manet, dum inculta senescit.

(10)　From the *Love Poems*, I.:
Love who will, for I'll love none;
There's fools enough beside me. . .
Then may she sigh, and lie alone,
In love with all, but lov'd of none.

This is reminiscent, in form and theme, of *Carm.* viii:

> Miser Catulle, desinas ineptire. . .
> At tu dolebis, cum rogaberis nulla. . .
> Quis nunc te adibit? cui videberis bella?

(11)   From *An Epistle*, "Dear Soul, the Time is Come and We Must Part":
> The amorous vine with wanton interlaces
> Clips still the tough elm in her kind embraces;

For this familiar figure of the vine and the elm, see *Carm.* lxii, 49-56, quoted in (9) above.

WILLIAM DRUMMOND OF HAWTHORNDEN
(1585-1649)

Drummond's sources are Italian and French rather than Latin; he was primarily a magnificent imitator of the poets of the Pléiade and of the florid Italian school. He is of the school of Spenser, not of the school of Donne; his poetry is "Italianate, florid, and fluent, not condensed, abrupt, and metaphysical."[1] Kastner's splendidly annotated edition of the Scottish poet shows how deeply indebted he was to the Italians and to them above all; his creative genius was small, and his capacity for imitation and paraphrase great; Professor Carpenter speaks rather cavalierly of "the elaborate and conscious prettinesses of Marinists like Drummond."[2]

Drummond's acquaintance with classical literature was not small, however; indeed, in his library, select yet comparatively large, the books in Latin outnumber those in any other language; Masson gives the interesting list: 267 books in Latin, 35 in Greek, 11 in Hebrew, 61 in Italian, 120 in French, 8 in Spanish, and 50 in English.[3] He points out, however, what is indubitably true, that "the French and Italian books. . . must represent, and beyond the proportion of their mere numbers, much favorite reading that was not of the Greek or Latin sort."[4] Surely, at any rate, the influence of the poet of our study is far less, indeed, infinitely less, than that of such poets as Marino or Ariosto. That Drummond knew Catullus, and that he knew him at first hand, is sure, but, not infrequently, when we trace the influence of Catullus in Drummond's works, we find the specific intermediary agency of an Italian or French poet. In my thirteenth quotation, for example, *A Translation of the Death of a Sparrow*, the source is unquestionably the two "sparrow" poems of Catullus, but Drummond's immediate source is a poem of the Frenchman Passerat.

(1)   From *Sonnet xxii* (Kastner, I, p. 24):
    Nymphs, sister Nymphs, which haunt this crystal brook. . .
    Whether ye garlands for your locks provide,
    Or pearly letters seek in sandy book,
    Or count your loves when Thetis was a bride?

This, as Kastner points out (Vol. I, p. 187), is an adaptation of a sonnet by Garcilaso, "*Hermosas ninfas, qui en el río metidas*"; the reference to Thetis is not in Garcilaso, however, and may be an echo of *Carm.* lxiv, 16-17, 19-20:

    Illa, siqua alia, viderunt luce marinas
    Mortales oculis nudato corpore nymphas. . .
    Tum Thetidis Peleus incensus fertur amore,
    Tum Thetis humanos non despexit hymenaeos.

(2)   From *Sonnet xxvii* (Kastner, I, p. 27):
    Let them have that [Aonian bays] who tuning sweetest lays
    By Tempe sit, or Aganippe well.

---

1   Grierson, *The First Half of the Seventeenth Century*, p. 149.
2   F. I. Carpenter, *English Lyric Poetry, 1500-1700*, p. lvii.
3   David Masson, *Drummond of Hawthornden*, p. 19.
4   *Ibid.*, p. 19.

Sidney has, in *Astrophel and Stella*, Sonnet lxxiv, the lines
> I never drank of Aganippe's well,
> Nor never did in shade of Tempe sit,

but Drummond may well have found his source in *Carm.* lxi, 29-30:
> Nympha quos super irrigat
> Frigerans Aganippe.

    (3)   From *Sonnet xxxv* (Kastner, I, p. 31):
> The Hyperborean hills, Ceraunus snow,
> Or Arimaspus (cruel) first thee bred,
> The Caspian tigers with their milk thee fed,
> And Fauns did human blood on thee bestow.

Kastner points out (I, p. 193) that this is adapted from Marino:
> Te l'Hiperboreo monte, ò l' Arimaspe,
>   Produsse, Elpinia, il Caucaso, ò 'l Cerauno. . .

but Marino may have been influenced by *Carm.* lxiv, 154-156:
> Quaenam te genuit sola sub rupe leaena,
> Quod mare conceptum spumantibus exspuit undis,
> Quae Syrtis, quae Scylla rapax, quae vasta Charybdis?

    (4)   From *Sonnet xxxvii* (Kastner, I, p. 34):
> Look how that elm this ivy doth embrace,
> And binds, and clasps with many a wanton fold.

For the familiar simile see *Carm.* lxii, 49-55, already quoted several times.

    (5)   From *Sonnet xl* (Kastner, I, p. 36):
> I die (dear Life) unless to me be given
> As many kisses as the spring hath flow'rs,
> Or as the silver drops of Iris' show'rs,
> Or as the stars in all-embracing Heaven.

For the general manner of the simile see *Carm.* vii, and for a specific borrowing note especially line 7,
> Aut quam sidera multa, cum tacet nox. . .

already several times quoted.

    (6)   From *Sonnet xlviii* (Kastner, I, p. 42):
> Yet Hair, for you, O that I were a Heaven!
>   Like Berenice's lock that ye might shine
> (But brighter far) about this arm of mine.

A clear reference to the *Coma Berenices*, *Carm.* lxvi.

    (7)   From *Sonnet v*, Part 2 (Kastner, I, p. 53):
> I have nought left to wish, my hopes are dead,
> And all with her beneath a marble laid.

See, for a possible source, *Carm.* lxviii, 94-95:
> Tecum una tota est nostra sepulta domus,
> Omnia tecum una perierunt gaudia nostra.

(8)   From *Song* 1 (Kastner,I, p. 58):
      Woods cut again do grow,
      Bud doth the rose and daisy, winter done,
      But we, once dead, no more do see the sun.
Perhaps an echo of the familiar theme of *Carm.* v:
      Soles occidere et redire possunt, etc.

(9)   *Upon the Death of a Linnet* (Kastner, I, p. 102):
      If cruel Death had ears,
      Or could be pleas'd by songs?
      This wing'd musician liv'd had many years,
      And Chloris mine had never wept these wrongs:
      For when it first took breath,
      The heavens their notes did unto it bequeath;
      And (if that Samian's sentence be found true)
      Amphion in this body liv'd of new:
      But Death, for that he nothing spares, nought hears,
      As he doth kings, it kill'd, O grief! O tears!
This is clearly inspired by *Carm.* iii, on the death of Lesbia's sparrow, though the thought and manner are alike sadly adulterate.

(10)   *Kisses Desired* (Kastner, I, p. 106):
      Though I with strange desire
      To kiss those rosy lips am set on fire,
      Yet will I cease to crave
      Sweet touches in such store,
      As he who long before
      From Lesbia them in thousands did receive.
      Heart mine, but once me kiss,
      And I by that sweet bliss
      Even swear to cease you to importune more;
      Poor one no number is:
      Another word of me ye shall not hear,
      After one kiss, but still one kiss, my dear.
This shows clearly Drummond's acquaintance with *Carm.* v and vii, already quoted.

(11)   *To Thaumantia* (Kastner, I, p. 119):
      Come, let us live, and love,
      And kiss, Thaumantia mine,
      I shall the elm be, be to me the vine.
      Come let us teach new billing to the dove:
      Nay, to augment our bliss,
      Let souls even other kiss,
      Let Love a workman be,
      Undo, distemper, and his cunning prove;
      Of kisses three make one, of one make three:

Though moon, sun, stars, be bodies far more bright,
Let them not vaunt they match us in delight.
This is imitated directly from Tasso:
Viviamo, amiamci, ò mia gradita Hielle,
    Hedra sia tu, che il caro tronco abbraccia;
but the ultimate source is Catullus, *Carm.* v, and, for the simile of the vine, *Carm.*
lxii, already mentioned in this chapter (4).

(12)   From *A Pastoral Elegie on the Death of S. Antonye Alexander* (Kastner,
II, p. 141):
    ——O Death! what treasure in one hour
Hast thou dispersed? How dost thou devour
What we on earth hold dearest? All things good,
Too envious heavens, how blast ye in the bud?
The poem is, as Kastner shows, directly influenced in the main by Baldassar
Castiglione's pastoral elegy *Alcon* (Kastner, II, p. 363):
Quis Deus, aut quis te casus miser abstulit? ergo
Optima quaeque rapit duri inclementia fati?
Ergo bonis tantum est aliquod male numen amicum;
but there is, to my mind, a very distinct echo of *Carm.* iii, 13-14:
At vobis male sit, malae tenebrae
Orci, quae omnia bella devoratis.
(13)   *Ibid.* (Kastner, II, p. 142):
But wretch, what wish I? To the winds I send
These plaints and prayers.
See *Carm.* lxiv, 164-165:
Sed quid ego ignaris nequiquam conqueror auris,
Exsternata malo?

(14)   From *A Translation of the Death of a Sparrow, out of Passerat* (Kastner,
II, p. 212-213):
Ah! if ye ask (my friends) why this salt shower
My blubbered eyes upon this paper pour,
Dead is my sparrow; he whom I did train,
And turn'd so toward, by a cat is slain.
Skipping no more now shall he on me attend.
Light displeaseth: would my days could end!
I'll hear no more him chirp forth pretty lays;
Have I not cause to curse my wretched days?. . .
The little body of a sparrow brave
In a foul gluttonous chat's womb clos'd remains,
Whose ghost now graceth the Elysian plains.
This poem is, as the title indicates, a translation of one by Passerat:
Demandez vous, amis, d' où viennent tant de larmes?. . .
Mon Passereau est mort, qui fut si bien appris;
but the ultimate source is unquestionably Catullus's two "sparrow poems," *Carmina*
ii and iii.

RICHARD CRASHAW
(1613?-1649)

The body of Crashaw's secular poetry is comparatively small, but, in what little of it there is, the influence of Catullus is rather considerable. Crashaw's "fine rapture" is akin to that of Catullus; his verse pours forth from him, as Catullus's did, in a fiery, passionate burst; and, vitiated though it may be by its occasional monstrous conceits and far-drawn fancies, it is always lyrical, always passionate, always the utterance of the heart rather than the lucubration of the brain. In reading Crashaw one is carried along by the very vehemence of the poet's feelings, just as one is swept along by the best verse of Catullus. The translation of the *Vivamus* is, to my mind, not so good as that of such an inferior poet as Alexander Brome; such phrases as "we, dark sons of sorrow," and "shuts the eyes of our short light" are as foreign to the spirit of Catullus's poem as anything well could be; Crashaw's own poetic rapture was too great to allow him to follow closely in the wake of another poet.

(1)   From *To The Queen* (Tutin, p. 197):

> Long may'st thou, laden with such clusters, lean
> Upon thy royal elm (fair vine!) and when
> The heavens will stay no longer, may thy glory
> And name dwell sweet in some eternal story!

For the simile see the lines in *Carm.* lxii, 49-50, 54, already quoted:

> Ut vidua in nudo vitis quae nascitur arvo
> Nunquam se extollit, nunquam mitem educat uvam. . .
> . . . Si forte eadem est ulmo coniuncta marito. . .

For a parallel passage, see *Carm.* lxi, 106-109.

(2)   *Out of Catullus* (Tutin, p. 208):

> Come and let us love, my dear,
> Let us love and never fear
> What the sourest fathers say:
> Brightest Sol that dies today
> Lives again as blithe tomorrow;
> But if we, dark sons of sorrow,
> Set, O then how long a Night
> Shuts the eyes of our short light!
> Then let amorous kisses dwell
> On our lips, begin and tell
> A thousand, and a hundred score,
> An hundred and a thousand more,
> Till another thousand smother
> That, and that wipe off another.
> Thus at last when we have numbered
> Many a thousand, many a hundred,
> We'll confound the reckoning quite
> And lose ourselves in wild delight:

While our joys so multiply
As shall mock the envious eye.

This is a translation of the many-times-translated *Carm.* v. The difficult task of making Catullus's "arithmetic" poetical in English is, to my mind, very gracefully accomplished by Crashaw, but he seems to have missed the point of the Latin in his concluding lines.

(3) From *In The Holy Nativity of our Lord God* (Tutin, p. 72):
> To Thee, meek Majesty! soft King
> Of *simple Graces and sweet Loves.*

Perhaps a faint, admittedly very faint, echo of Catullus's *Veneres Cupidinesque*, *Carm.* iii, 1.

(4) From *Alexias*, Elegy I (Tutin, p. 148):
> The noted sea shall change his name with me;
> I 'mongst the blest stars a new name shall be;
>
> . . . .
>
> O live, so rare a love! live! and in thee
> The too frail life of female constancy.
> Farewell; and shine, fair soul, shine there above,
> Firm in thy crown, as here fast in thy love.

Perhaps these passages were suggested by the *Coma Berenices*, *Carm.* lxvi.

(5) From *Alexias*, Elegy II, (Tutin, p. 149):
> For thee I talk to trees; with silent groves
> Expostulate my woes and much wrong'd loves;
> Hills and relentless rocks, or if there be
> Things that in hardness more allude to thee,
> To these I talk in tears, and tell my pain,
> And answer too for them in tears again.

This complaint of a deserted wife bears a considerable resemblance to the lament of the forsaken Ariadne; see *Carm.* lxiv, 164-166:
> Sed quid ego ignaris nequiquam conqueror auris,
> Exsternata malo, quae nullis sensibus auctae
> Nec missas audire queunt nec reddere voces?. . .

GILES FLETCHER
(1588?-1623)
PHINEAS FLETCHER
(1582-1650)

Very little of the verse of Giles Fletcher is in any sense lyrical; there is, so far as I could discover, no reference to Catullus in the shorter poems which I have examined. It is probable enough that the poet of *Christ's Triumph and Victorie* had no knowledge of Catullus; if he had any such knowledge, his subject matter was not of a nature to permit easily of his using it.

Phineas Fletcher seems to have had some knowledge of Catullus; the evidences of this knowledge are most patent in an epithalamium of his, which seems to bear rather clear indications of an acquaintance with at least one of Catullus's epithalamia. Phineas Fletcher's work is, in the main, not lyrical, and, like his brother's, not of a nature to permit of the display of classical learning. Fletcher's mind was didactic and, in a slightly perverted sense of the word, scientific; the school to which the two brothers belonged was "essentially narrative, allegorical and diffuse, and given to the cult of nature in her gentle aspects. There was not much place for the lyric among them."[1]

(1)   From Song, in *Sicelides*, V. 6 (Boas, I, p. 262):
Hymen, Hymen, come saffron Hymen.
That love for ever constant stands
Where hearts are tied before the hands. . .
Hymen, Hymen, come saffron Hymen.
For the form of the invocation see *Carm.* lxii, 5:
Hymen o Hymenaee, Hymen ades o Hymenaee,
and for "saffron Hymen," see *Carm.* lxi, 8:
Flammeum cape.
The *flammeum* was really "saffron" (*luteum*) in color; see Lucan, *Pharsalia*, II, 361:
Lutea demissos velarunt flammea vultus.

(2)   *An Hymen at the Marriage of my most deare Cousins Mr. W. and M. R.* (Boas, II, 223-225):
This poem is unquestionably influenced by the 61st and 62d *Carmina* (the Epithalamia) of Catullus; this influence is, perhaps, most noticeable in the imitation of the constantly recurring Catullian refrain:
Hymen, oh Hymen, here thy saffron garment bring,
and, for another example,
Hymen, come Hymen; here thy saffron coat is rested.
For these see (1) above. For such a refrain as
Hymen, come holy Hymen; Hymen loud they sing,
see the injunction to the maidens, *Carm.* lxi, 38-40:
——Agite in modum;
Dicite, 'O Hymenaee Hymen,
O Hymen Hymenaee.'

1   Schelling, *The English Lyric*, p. 81.

For
        Hymen, come Hymen, now untie the maiden zone,
see *Carm.* lxi, 52-53:
        Tibi virgines
        Zonula solvunt sinus.
    The praise of Hymen in this poem, while not following the phrases of Catullus, is clearly inspired by them:
        Hymen, the tier of hearts already tied;
        Hymen, the end of lovers never ending;
        Hymen the cause of joys, joys never tried;
        Joys never to be spent, yet ever spending. . .
        Warrant of lovers, the true sea of loving,
        Sign'd with the face of joy; the holy knot,
        That binds two hearts, and holds from slippery moving;
        A gainful loss, a stain without a blot.
See *Carm.* lxi, 46-75, for a passage very similar to this in spirit, but too long for quotation.
    The description of Hymen is clearly Catullian:
        See where he goes, how all the troop he cheereth,
        Clad with a saffron coat, in's hand a light;
        In all his brow not one sad cloud appeareth:
        His coat all pure, his torch all burning bright.
    The "saffron coat" has been discussed in (1) above; for the "flaming torch" see *Carm.* lxi, 14-15:
        Manu
        Pineam quate taedam.

    (3)   From *On Women's Lightness* (Boas, II, p. 239):
        Fond thoughts, fond heart, fond hope; but fondest I,
        To grasp the wind, and love inconstancy!
    The comparison of a woman's words and actions to the constancy of the shifting wind may be reminiscent of *Carm.* lxx, 3-4:
        . . . Sed mulier cupido quod dicit amanti
        In vento et rapida scribere oportet aqua.

WILLIAM HABINGTON
(1605-1654)

The lyric powers of William Habington, the "Catholic puritan",[1] were not great—he sings in a low-pitched, uncertain strain, sweetly enough, indeed, in the main, but, all too often, with a mawkish sweetness. "In Habington,"says an old editor, Elton, with what to him was high, but to us, dubious praise, "In Habington we have no burning blisses, or blasphemous exclamations of delirious rapture. Still less is the lady insulted by vaunts of a general or systematic sensuality. She is neither complimented by the assurance of dividing the thoughts of her lover with the vulgar pleasures of the glass, nor told that between kisses and bumpers life glides pleasantly away. Instead of this, we hear the delicacy of sentiment with which our mothers were pleased to be addressed, and to which our daughters may lend their ear, without risk of mental contamination."[2] Habington is, indeed, not so bad as we might fear him to be from his editor's eulogy, nor, in the main, do I think he deserves Professor Grierson's adjectives "tedious" and "thin-blooded."[3] Professor Schelling thinks that he can discern in *Castara* something of the "larger utterance of earlier days,"[4] and certainly, to my mind, his poems have a certain real sweetness and charm. But whatever his qualities, no one could be further divorced in spirit from the fiery, passionate-souled Catullus than the Platonic, moralizing lover of Castara. What traces of a Catullian influence I can find in this poet are slight enough, and, in certain of my quotations, at any rate, somewhat doubtful. The fifth example, with its curiously interesting inversion of Catullian sentiment, shows fairly conclusively, to my mind, that Habington was acquainted with Catullus.

(1)   From *To Castara* (Elton, p. 134):
> How happy in this state the humble vine
> Doth 'bout some taller tree herself entwine
> And so grows fruitful.

For this familiar simile, see *Carm.* lxii, 49-55:
> Ut vidua in nudo vitis quae nascitur arvo. . .
> . . . Si forte eadem est ulmo coniuncta marito,
> Multi illam agricolae, multi accoluere iuvenci.

(2)   From *To Death, Castara Being Sick* (Elton, p. 182):
> Court her gently, learn to prove
> Nimble in the thefts of love.

See *Carm.* vii, 8, for a parallel:
> Furtivos hominum vident amores.

(3)   From *To a Friend, Inviting Him to a Meeting upon Promise* (Elton, p. 190):

---

1   Grierson, *The Background of English Literature*, p. 142.
2   Charles A. Elton's edition of Habington's *Castara*, pp. 7-8.
3   Grierson, *op. cit.*, p. 141.
4   Schelling, *The English Lyric*, p. 86.

> Come, then, and bring with you, prepared for fight
> Unmixt Canary. . . .
> . . . My sack will disengage
> All humane thoughts.

This bears a considerable likeness, in matter and form, to *Carm.* xiii:

> Cenabis bene, mi Fabulle, apud me. . .
> Si tecum attuleris bonam atque magnam
> Cenam. . .
> Sed contra accipies meros amores. . .
> Nam unguentum dabo. . . .

(4)   From *To Castara, upon an Embrace* (Elton, p. 237):

> 'Bout the husband oak the vine
>   Thus wreathes to kiss his leavy face.

See the passage referred to and quoted in (1).

(5)   From *To Castara, the Reward of Innocent Love:*

> Time's ever ours, while we despise
> The sensual idol of our clay;
> For though the Sun doth rise and set,
> We joy one everlasting day.

This is, in my opinion, a very interesting case of what we may call inverse influence or influence by repulsion. Habington takes the familiar Catullian thought, *Carm.* v, 4-6:

> Soles occidere et redire possunt:
> Nobis, cum semel occidit brevis lux,
> Nox est perpetua una dormienda,

and turns it, as it were, inside out, using it to refute the pessimistic hedonism of the Latin poet.

RICHARD LOVELACE
(1618-1658)

Lovelace's education was perfunctory and uncertain, but it filled him at least with a profound reverence for the classics. Strangely enough, the poets whom he came most to admire (if imitation and translation be indications of admiration) were the poles asunder: "He does not," says Hartman, "appear to have been a deeply learned man, though he had . . . a superficial acquaintance with the classics, especially with such poets as Catullus and Ausonius."[1] The traces of Catullus are frequent even in his independent poems; it is by his translations, however, that he makes his knowledge of the Latin poet most apparent. His manner of choosing poems of Catullus for translation is most interesting, in that it passes human understanding; now he chooses a lovely poem of mournful yet tender recrimination, now he translates a stupid and only half-intelligible paederastic epigram, and again he turns into English a vulgar epigram leveled against a brothel-keeper. Yet this uncertainty of judgment in the choice of what is good is characteristic of the poet. Lovelace, says Schelling, is a poet "of great inequality. He varies between two or three perfect little songs. . . sure of a place in any anthology including his time, and poems that fall into mere slovenliness and unintelligibility."[2] So, in like manner, his use of Catullus varies between grace and delicacy of judgment and indiscriminate choice of the poorest and least characteristic of Catullus's poems.

(1)　From *The Apostacy of One, and But One Lady* (Caxton Club ed., I, p. 66):
　　　Oh, she is constant as the wind,
　　　　That revels in the ev'ning's air . . .
For a parallel see *Carm*. lxx, 3-4, already quoted.

(2)　From *Amarantha, a Pastorall* (C. C. ed., I, p. 80):
　　　Weep, all ye Graces, and you sweet
　　　　Quire, that at the hill inspir'd meet. . .
Perhaps suggested by *Carm*. iii, 1-2:
　　　Lugete, O Veneres Cupidinesque,
　　　　Et quantum est homines venustiorum!

(3)　From *Princesse Loysa Drawing* (C. C. ed., I, p. 107):
　　　Theseus return'd invokes the air
　　　And winds, then wafts his fair;
　　　Whilst Ariadne ravish't stood
　　　Half in his arms, half in the flood.
This description of Ariadne "half in the flood" seems drawn from *Carm*. lxiv, 128-129:
　　　Tum tremuli salis adversas procurrere in undas
　　　　Mollia nudatae tollentem tegmina surae.
and *Carm*. lxiv, 66-67:
　　　Omnia quae toto delapsa e corpore passim
　　　　Ipsius ante pedes fluctus salis adludebant.

1　Cyril Hughes Hartman, *The Cavalier Spirit*, p. 118.
2　Schelling, *The English Lyric*, p. 91.

(4)   From *The Triumphs of Philamore and Amoret* (C. C. ed., II, p. 79):
> The twice-born god, still gay and ever young,
> With ivy crown'd, first leads the glorious throng:
> He Ariadne's starry coronet
>   Designs for th' brighter beams of Amoret.

Perhaps inspired by the description of Bacchus leading his votaries, *Carm.* lxiv, 251-253:

> At parte ex alia florens volitabat Iacchus
> Cum thiaso satyrorum et Nysigenis silenis
> Te quaerens, Ariadna, tuoque incensus amore.

(5)   From *An Anniversary of the Hymenaeals of . . . Thos. Stanley* (C. C. ed., II, p. 96):
> Come then, pale virgins, roses strow . . . .
> You too may hope the same seraphic joy,
>   Old time cannot destroy,
>   Nor fulness cloy.

For a similar cheering promise see *Carm.* lxi, 36-38:

> Vosque item simul, integrae
> Virgines, quibus advenit
> Par dies. . . .

(6)   From *On Sanazar's Being Honored with Six Hundred Duckets. by the Clarissimi of Venice* (C. C. ed., II, p. 104):
> The eternal laurel. . . .
> Like to the golden tripod, it did pass
> From this to this, till't came to him, whose 'twas,
> Caesar to Gallus trundled it, and he
> To Maro: Maro, Naso, unto thee?
> Naso to his Tibullus flung the wreath,
> He to Catullus: thus did each bequeath.

These verses throw an interesting and curious light upon Lovelace's knowledge, or ignorance, of the literary history of Rome. He does place Caesar before Vergil in point of time, but Catullus later, by two removes, than Vergil! He could not have confused his dates more scandalously. But this is apparent, that he considers Catullus as marking the apogee of Latin poetry; to him at last the laurel comes, "to him, whose 'twas."

(7)   *Ad M. T. Ciceronem* (C. C. ed., II, p. 132):
> Tully, to thee, Rome's eloquent sole heir,
> The best of all that are, shall be, and were,
> I the worst poet send my best thanks of pray'r;
> Ev'n by how much the worst of poets I,
> By so much you the best of patrons be.

A translation of *Carm.* xlix:

> Disertissime Romuli nepotum,
> Quot sunt quotque fuere, Marce Tulli,

Quotque post aliis erunt in annis,
Gratias tibi maximas Catullus
Agit pessimus omnium poeta,
Tanto pessimus omnium poeta
Quanto tu optimus omnium patronus.

(8)   *Ad Iuvencium* (C. C. ed., II, p. 133):
Juvencius, thy fair sweet eyes
If to my fill that I may kiss,
Three hundred thousand times I'd kiss,
Nor future age should cloy this bliss;
No, not if thicker than ripe ears
The harvest of our kisses bears.

A translation of *Carm.* xlviii:
Mellitos oculos tuos, Iuventi,
Siquis me sinat usque basiare,
Usque ad milia basiem trecenta,
Nec unquam videar satur futurus,
Non si densior aridis aristis
Sit nostrae seges osculationis.

(9)   *De Puero et Praecone* (C. C. ed., II, p. 134):
With a fair boy a crier we behold,
What should we think, but he would not be sold?

On this bad translation of a pointless paederastic "epigram" we have already commented; see *Carm.* cvi:
Cum puero bello praeconem qui videt esse,
Quid credat, nisi se vendere discupere?

(10)   *Ad Fabullum* (C. C. ed., II, p. 149):
Fabullus, I will treat you handsomely
Shortly, if the kind gods will favor thee.
If thou dost bring with thee a del'cate mess,
An olio or so, a pretty lass,
Brisk wine, sharp tales, all sorts of drollery,
These if thou bringst (I say) along with thee,
You shall feed highly, friend: for, know, the ebbs
Of my lank purse are full of spiders' webs;
But then, again, you shall receive clear love,
Or what more grateful or more sweet may prove:
For with an ointment I will favor thee
My Venus's and Cupids gave to me,
Of which, once smelt, the gods thou wilt implore,
Fabullus, that they'd make you nose all o'er.

A rather charming translation of a charming little poem, *Carm.* xiii—a few lines will show the closeness of the translation:
Cenabis bene, mi Fabulle, apud me
Paucis, si tibi di favent, diebus,

Si tecum attuleris bonam atque magnam
Cenam, non sine candida puella,
Et vino et sale et omnibus cachinnis.
Haec si, inquam, attuleris, venuste noster,
Cenabis bene. . . . .

(11)   *In Rufum* (C. C. ed., II, p. 157):
That no fair woman will, wonder not why,
Clap (Rufus) under thine her tender thigh;
Not a silk gown shall once melt one of them,
Nor the delights of a transparent gem.
A scurvy story kills thee, which doth tell,
That in thy armpits a fierce goat doth dwell.
Him they all fear full of an ugly stench;
Nor 's 't fit he should lie with a handsome wench;
Wherefore this noses cursed plague first crush,
Or cease to wonder, why they fly you thus.

A close translation of a worthless poem, *Carm.* lxix; a few lines will indicate the closeness of the translation:

Noli admirari quare tibi femina nulla,
    Rufe, velit tenerum supposuisse femur,
Non si illam rarae labefactes munere vestis
    Aut perluciduli deliciis lapidis. . . .

(12)   *De Inconstantia Foeminei Amoris* (C. C. ed., II, p. 158):
My mistress says she'll marry none but me;
No, not if Jove himself a suitor be.
She says so; but what women say to kind
Lovers, we write in rapid streams and wind.

A neat translation of *Carm.* lxx, already several times quoted.

(13)   *Ad Lesbiam* (C. C. ed., II, p. 159):
That me alone you lov'd, you once did say,
Nor should I to the king of gods give way.
Then I loved thee not as a common dear,
But as a father doth his children cheer.
Now thee I know, more bitterly I smart;
Yet thou to me more light and cheaper art.
What pow'r is this? that such a wrong should press
Me to love more, but wish thee well much less.
I hate and love; wouldst thou the reason know?
I know not; but I burn, and feel it so.

All but the last two lines form a translation of *Carm.* lxxii:

Dicebas quondam solum te nosse Catullum,
    Lesbia, nec prae me velle tenere Iovem.
Dilexi tum te non ut vulgus amicam,
    Sed pater ut gnatos diligit et generos. . .

The last two lines translate *Carm*. lxxxv:

> Odi et amo. Quare id faciam fortasse requiris.
> Nescio, sed fieri sentio et excrucior.

(14) *In Lesbiam* (C. C. ed., II, p. 160):

> By thy fault is my mind brought to that pass,
> That it its office quite forgotten has:
> For be'est thou best, I cannot wish thee well,
> And be'est thou worst, then I must love thee still.

A translation of *Carm*. lxxv:

> Huc est mens deducta tua, mea Lesbia, culpa,
>   Atque ita se officio perdidit ipsa suo,
> Ut iam nec bene velle queat tibi, si optuma fias,
>   Ne desistere amare, omnia si facias.

(15) *Ad Quintium* (C. C. ed., II, p. 161):

> Quintius, if you'll endear Catullus' eyes,
> Or what he dearer than his eyes doth prize,
> Ravish not what is dearer than his eyes,
> Or what he dearer than his eyes doth prize.

A very close translation of *Carm*. lxxxii. The parallel arrangement in the two couplets, touching and lovely in the Latin, is in English rhyme singularly unpleasant:

> Quinti, si tibi vis oculos debere Catullum
> Aut aliquid si quid carius est oculis,
> Eripere ei noli multo quod carius illi
> Est oculis, seu quid carius est oculis.

(16) *De Quintia et Lesbia* (C. C. ed., II, p. 162):

> Quintia is handsome, fair, tall, straight: all these
> Very particulars I grant with ease:
> But she all ore's not handsome: here's her fault:
> In all that bulk there's not one corn of salt,
> Whilst Lesbia, fair and handsome too all ore,
> All graces and all wit from all hath bore.

A good terse translation of *Carm*. lxxxvi:

> Quintia formosa est multis, mihi candida, longa,
>   Recta est. Haec ego sic singula confiteor,
> Totum illud 'formosa' nego: nam nulla venustas,
>   Nulla in tam magno est corpore mica salis.
> Lesbia formosa est, quae cum pulcherrima tota est,
>   Tum omnibus una omnis subripuit Veneres.

(17) *De Suo in Lesbia Amore* (C. C. ed., II, p. 163):

> No one can boast herself so much belov'd,
> Truly as Lesbia my affections prov'd;
> No faith was ere with such a firm knot bound,
> As in my love on my part I have found.

An ungraceful translation of *Carm.* lxxxvii:

> Nulla potest mulier tantum se dicere amatam
>> Vere, quantum a me Lesbia amata mea es:
> Nulla fides ullo fuit unquam in foedere tanta
>> Quanta in amore tuo ex parte reperta mea est.

(18)   *Ad Sylonem* (C. C. ed., II, p. 164):

> Sylo, pray pay me my ten sesterces,
> Then rant and roar as much as you shall please;
> Or if that money takes you, pray, give ore
> To be a pimp, or else to rant and roar.

A translation of an uninteresting epigram, *Carm.* ciii:

> Aut sodes mihi redde decem sestertia, Silo,
>> Deinde esto quamvis saevus et indomitus:
> Aut, si te nummi delectant, desine quaeso
>> Leno esse atque idem saevus et indomitus.

These, then, are such instances as we can discover of the influence of Catullus upon Lovelace, an influence marked but not pervasive, strong and yet but rarely happy. When his brother, Dudley Posthumus, sought a motto to preface the various elegies on Lovelace composed by his friends, he turned to Catullus, and addressed the dead poet in those exquisitely lovely and pathetic words with which Catullus himself had mourned his departed brother:

> Nunquam ego te, vita frater amabilior,
> Adspiciam posthac? at certe semper amabo.

ALEXANDER BROME
(1620-1666)

The classical influence upon Alexander Brome is very slight, extending, in the main, as it does, only to commonplace and trite mythological references. He is primarily a maker of rollicking drinking songs and of not too delicately barbed verses against the Puritans, more of a rhymester than a poet. Yet in the midst of these drinking songs and Cavalier verses we find one rather graceful paraphrase of the *Vivamus, mea Lesbia* of Catullus. With Brome, to be sure, the verses have lost most of their poignancy and passion; they lilt along carelessly and nimbly enough, but the shallow Cavalier has succeeded in distilling all real feeling out of them. The verses, however, are unquestionably not infelicitous.

(1)   From *Songs: Courtship* (Chalmers, VI, pp. 649-650):

My Lesbia, let us live and love,
    Let crabbed age talk what it will:
The Sun, though down, returns above,
    But we, once dead, must so be still.

Kiss me a thousand times, and then
    Give me a hundred kisses more;
Now kiss a thousand times again,
    Then t' other hundred as before.

Come, a third thousand, and to those
    Another hundred kisses fix;
That done, to make the sweeter close,
    We'll millions of kisses mix.

And huddle them together so,
    That we ourselves shan't know how many;
And others can't their number know,
    If we should envi'd be by any.

But then, when we have done all this,
    That our pleasures may remain,
We'll continue on our bliss,
    By unkissing all again.

Thus we'll love and thus we'll live,
    While our posting minutes fly,
We'll have no time to vex or grieve,
    But kiss and unkiss till we die.

See *Carm.* v.

GEORGE WITHER
(1588-1667)

The classical strain in Wither is comparatively slight; indeed, he takes pains to declare his refusal to mould himself upon the ancients:

> Pedants shall not tie my strains
> To our antique poets' veins,
> As if we, in latter days,
> Knew to love, but not to praise.
> Being born as free as these,
> I will sing as I shall please.[1]

Professor Grierson has pointed out that such a poem as *Fidelia* is modeled upon the Epistles of Ovid,[2] and unquestionably it is with Ovid, of all the Latin poets, that he has most in common. There is no absolute certainty that he knew Catullus at all; indeed, the testimony of silence is against his having done so; when, for example, he wishes to mention fair ladies who have found immortality in the verse of their lovers, the name of Lesbia does not come to him at all:

> Though the much-commended Celia,
> Lovely Laura, Stella, Delia,
> Who in former times excell'd,
> Live in lines unparallel'd. . . . .[3]

Long though Wither's poems may be, they are still essentially lyrical in strain; Professor Grierson speaks justly of the "high enthusiasm for moral goodness, for nature, and for song, with a more ardent love-strain, uttered in a sweet but shriller music,"[4] which characterize Wither's best poetry and make it prevailingly lyrical.

(1) *Fidelia* is concerned, like the Ariadne episode in *Carm.* lxiv, with the grief of a lovely woman abandoned by the man whom she had believed in and loved. There are indubitable likenesses between the complaints of Fidelia and of Ariadne, but it is impossible to establish any certain debt of the English poet to the Latin; what resemblances there are may be purely adventitious; each has imagined a tenderly-reared, sensitive, and beautiful young woman deserted and forlorn; if they speak alike, it is not necessary to accuse the later poet of imitation; each speaks the language of the heart, and that language, in similar circumstances, is alike with Fidelia and Ariadne. One radical difference there is between the two young women, however: Ariadne has been betrayed, but she cares little about the moral consequences of her betrayal; Fidelia is happily *intacta*, but she is greatly disturbed at the mere thought that there was once a possibility of her being seduced; the gap here is wide between Paganism and Puritanism. But, to repeat, there are unmistakable likenesses in the two poems, some of which it may be profitable to mention. Fidelia thinks with sorrow of the happy days before Love the disturber entered her life; such happiness Catullus claims for Ariadne also:

---

1 Wither, *Fair Virtue*, ll. 509-514 (Sidgwick, *Poetry of George Wither*, II, p. 27-8).
2 In the sixth of the Messenger Lectures at Cornell University, April 21, 1927 (not yet published).
3 Wither, *Fair Virtue*, ll. 289-292 (Sidgwick, II, p. 20).
4 Grierson, *First Half of the Seventeenth Century*, p. 145.

> Happy was I; yea, well it was with me,
> Before I came to be bewitch'd by thee.
> I joy'd the sweet'st content that ever maid
> Possessed yet; and truly well-a-paid,
> Made to myself alone as pleasant mirth
> As ever any virgin did on earth. (ll. 83-88)

She marvels, like Ariadne, at the changed countenance of the lover who has promised so much:

> Art thou
> So overcloyed with my favors now?
> Art wearied since with loving, and estranged
> So far? Is thy affection so much changed,
> That I of all my hopes must be deceived,
> And all good thoughts of thee be quite bereaved? (ll. 73-78)

The frailty of a lover's vow is to her, as to Ariadne, matter of the greatest wonder:

> Swear'st thou so deeply that thou wouldst persever,
> That I might thus be cast away forever? (ll. 467-8)

Just as Ariadne would have been willing to serve Theseus as a slave, if only she might be with him, so Fidelia would rejoice in the least favor of the faithless lover:

> And if thou wilt not be to me as when
> We first did love, do but come see me then;
> Vouchsafe that I may sometime with thee walk,
> Or sit and look on thee, or hear thee talk.
> And I that most content once aimed at
> Will think there is a world of bliss in that. (ll. 545-550)

Like Ariadne, too, Fidelia praises her past faithfulness:

> Ne'er was there one more true than I to thee,
> . . . . Though my fate must now despised be,
> Unpriz'd, unvalued at the lowest rate. (ll.705-7)

Finally, though she does not, like Ariadne, curse the faithless lover, she prophesies punishment for him:

> For though I wish not the least harm to thee,
> I fear, the just heavens will revenged be. (ll. 201-2)

These likenesses, I have said, may be purely adventitious; there is all the difference between Wither's long and wandering poem and the magnificent burst of lyric grief and indignation Catullus puts into the mouth of Ariadne that there is between a brisk but shallow brooklet and a swirling, headlong torrent. But, be this as it may, certain likenesses are indubitably present.

(2)   From the *Epithalamion for the Princess Elizabeth*, l. 155 (Sidgwick, I, p. 164):

> Yea, Hymen in his saffron-colored weed
> To celebrate his rites is full agreed.

For a possible source see *Carm.* lxi, 8-10, already several times quoted.

(3)   *Ibid.*, l. 189 (Sidgwick, I, p. 165-6):

> We hope that this will the uniting prove

Of countries and of nations by your love,
And that from out your blessed loins shall come
Another terror to the whore of Rome,
And such a stout Achilles as shall make
Her tottering walls and weak foundation shake,
For Thetis-like thy fortunes do require
Thy issue should be greater than his sire.

In like manner, in *Carm.* lxiv, the Fates prophesy to Thetis and Peleus the birth of Achilles, who shall be a terror to the city of Troy, 328 ff.; note in particular ll. 338-9:

Nascetur vobis expers terroris Achilles
Hostibus haud tergo, sed forti pectore notus.

(4) From *Fair Virtue*, l. 2059 (Sidgwick, II, p. 80)
This is she, in whom there meets
All variety of sweets;
An epitome of all
That on earth we fair may call.

For a like passage, see *Carm.* lxxxvi, 5-6:

Lesbia formosa est, quae cum pulcherrima tota est,
Tum omnibus una omnis subripuit Veneres.

ROBERT HERRICK
(1591-1674)

No English poet of the period we have been considering, indeed, no poet in the whole range of English literature, is more thoroughly acquainted with Catullus and more fully endowed with the superficial graces of Catullus than is Robert Herrick. He translates and paraphrases Catullus; he imitates him again and again; his poems are full of recondite suggestions of his familiarity with the Latin poet. He has the grace and sense of form which characterize Catullus; he has much of the Latin poet's attitude toward life, the pagan sense of the transitoriness of existence and the necessity of catching the joys of the passing hour. But with all this there is a very great difference between the two poets; Herrick is not "Catullian" in the more important sense which we attach to the word, that is, in the sense of possessing fiery earnestness and passionate ardor. In fundamental things the pleasure-loving, gracefully amorous lover of Julia and Anthea, of Biancha and Corinna, has little in common with the lover of Lesbia. Gosse puts the point succinctly when he decries "the same old blunder" of declaring Herrick to be of all English poets most like Catullus,—"Indeed," he says, "it would be difficult to name a lyric poet with whom he had less in common than the Veronese, whose eagle flights into the very noonday depths of passion . . . have no sort of fellowship with the pipings of our gentle and luxurious babbler by the flowery banks."[1] And he speaks, with equal justice, of the "total want of passion in Herrick's language about women,"[2] so different from the utter earnestness of Catullus. There is no absolute truth in Herrick's love poetry, no mastering reality. Moorman puts the contrast well: "There is no development in the poet's amours, no inrush of hot jealousy, no satiety, no quarreling, no reconciliation. The poet, in spite of his fourteen mistresses, has no rivals who seek to rob him of his love. We have, indeed, only to compare, in this respect, Herrick's mistress poems with those of other poets in whose case we know that the love and the loved ones are real, in order to appreciate this difference. Catullus's love for Lesbia can be traced exactly through its different stages—passionate yearning, full fruition, disillusionment, and jealousy, ending in bitter loathing—and something like this dramatic development is found in some of the love-poetry of the Elizabethan poets—for instance, in the love elegies of Donne."[3] This mention of Donne is significant, for he, with not a hundredth part of the knowledge of Catullus that Herrick had, possessed, as Professor Grierson well points out, far more of the fine passionate spirit of the Latin poet.[4]

But, different as the two poets are in nature, the debt of Herrick to Catullus is, as I have said, very great. "Of the Roman lyric poets," says Moorman, "it is Catullus and Horace that have made the deepest impression upon him"; and he goes on to point out that, considering only things external, "the *Hesperides* bear a striking superficial resemblance to the *Carmina* of Catullus in their disorderly arrangement—an arrangement which ignores chronological order, and brings the

---

1 Gosse, *Seventeenth Century Studies*, p. 136.
2 *Ibid.*, p. 120.
3 Moorman, *Robert Herrick, A Biographical and Critical Study*, p. 71.
4 Grierson, *Donne's Poetical Works*, II, pp. xlii-xliii.

loftiest strains of lyric song into closest proximity with the coarsest epigrams."[5] He remarks, too, upon the "striking sincerity of utterance which characterizes either poet," (excluding, as we have done, the love poems of Herrick), the "sympathetic nature" and "tender regard for friends and relations" of both poets, and the "passionate intensity" little short of that of Catullus, which Herrick sometimes displays,[6] instancing in particular his lines on his dying brother, lines poignant and true, to be sure, but bearing no mark at all of the direct influence of Catullus (see Moorman's edition, p. 73).

But there is another side to the matter. M. Delattre in his most excellent study of the English poet endeavors to minimize the influence of Catullus upon Herrick, and would controvert Lowell's striking dictum that Herrick is the "most Catullian of poets since Catullus,"[7] even in the matter of verbal influence. His opinions are worth quoting at some length. "On a attaché," says he, "beaucoup trop d'importance, croyons nous, à l'influence que Catulle aurait exercée sur Herrick." He then animadverts upon the assertions of W. C. Hazlitt, Grosart, Lowell, and Saintsbury that there is a very close likeness between the two poets, and goes on: "Or rien ne nous semble plus erroné. Les emprunts que Herrick fait au poète latin sont beaucoup moins nombreux qu'on n'a pris l'habitude de le dire, et surtout ne portent point sur ce qui constitue l'originalité essentielle de l'amant de Lesbie." He grants that "Herrick s'est évidemment inspiré des epithalames de Catulle, dont il ne réproduit cependant, dans ses propres odes nuptiales, que l'éclat extérieur, que le decor de légendes et de coutumes romaines, sans atteindre jamais à la sincérité vibrante du poète ancien." The undoubted translations of Catullus he brands as "fort mediocres," and contests a number of Grosart's claims of a Catullian influence in certain of Herrick's poems. Many of his strictures on Grosart's extravagant statements are well taken; he casts just doubt, for example, on Grosart's suggestion that two lines in *The Vision* (Moorman, p. 51):

> Her legs were such *Diana* shows,
> When *tuckt up* she a-hunting goes,

were borrowed by Herrick from *Carm.* lxiv, 128-129:

> Tum tremuli salis adversas procurrere in undas
> Mollia nudatae tollentem tegmina surae.

Here, of course, Delattre is entirely right, as he is also in questioning Grosart's attributing the matter of *Kissing Usury* (Moorman, p. 29) to the influence of *Carm.* v. His concluding sentences on this question are deserving of quotation, if only to strengthen what we have had to say about the differences between Catullus and Herrick: "Rien en effet n'est plus opposé à l'épicurisme aimable et satisfait de Herrick que la passion poignante de l'amant de Lesbie. L'un évoque en nous l'idée d'un homme d'âge moyen, toujours calme, raisonnable jusque dans les extravagances d'imagination; l'autre celle d'un jeune homme dont le coeur éperdu eut toujours vingt ans ... Catulle nous conte les milles aventures de son coeur fougueux, depuis les tendresses et orgueilleuses voluptés de son amour commençant jusqu'au le dégoût que lui inspire, par la suite, sa tyrannique passion, jusqu'aux sarcasmes enfin

5 Moorman, *op. cit.*, p. 213.
6 *Ibid.*, p. 214.
7 Lowell, *Among My Books*, "Lessing," p. 391.

et au mépris amer de ses billets d'adieu. Herrick est incapable de comprendre toute la grandeur de cet amour. Il s'arrête à la tendresse aimable et voulue des 'petits vers' de ce poète 'érudit,' à la souplesse élégante et comme un peu maniérée de certaines pièces, mais il ne se hausse point jusqu'à la simplicité passionnée qui emplit ce coeur véhément, et qui est la source essentielle des *Carmina*."[8] But, though I grant freely to M. Delattre that there are essential and most important differences between the two poets in sincerity and height of soul, I am firmly convinced that the influence of Catullus upon Herrick was far greater than he has indicated. In evidence I offer the following pages, which represent, perhaps, as careful, if not so able, a study of the influence of Catullus upon Herrick as either the studies of M. Delattre or Dr. Grosart:

(1) From *When He Would Have His Verses Read* (Moorman, p. 7):
When up the thyrse is rais'd, and when the sound
Of sacred orgies flies, a round, a round.

Pollard says (I, p. 260): "Herrick's glosses show that the passage he had in mind was Catullus, lxiv, 256-269:
Harum pars tecta quatiebant cuspide thyrsos,

. . . .

Pars obscura cavis celebrabant orgia cistis,
Orgia, quae frustra cupiunt audire profani."

(2) From *The Vine* (Moorman, p. 16):
I dream'd this mortal part of mine
Was metamorphos'd to a vine;
Which crawling one and every way,
Enthrall'd my dainty Lucia.
Methought, her long small legs and thighs
I with my tendrils did surprise;
Her belly, buttocks, and her waist
By my soft nervelets were embrac'd;
About her head I writhing hung,
And with rich clusters (hid among
The leaves) her temples I behung. . . .
But when I crept with leaves to hide
Those parts, which maids keep unespy'd,
Such fleeting pleasures there I took,
That with the fancy I awook;
And found (Ah me!) this flesh of mine
More like a stock, than like a vine.

This seems to be an amplification of Catullus's much-used simile, *Carm.* lxi, 106-109:
Lenta quin velut adsitas
Vitis implicat arbores,
Implicabitur in tuum
Complexum.

8 For this and the preceding quotations see Floris Delattre, *Robert Herrick, Contribution à l'étude de la poésie lyrique en Angleterre au dix-septième siècle*, pp. 408-410.

(3)   From *On Himself* (Moorman, p. 17):
    Young I was, but now am old,
    But I am not yet grown cold;
    I can play, and I can twine
    'Bout a virgin like a vine.
See quotation from *Carm.* lxi, in (2).

(4)   From *Again* (Moorman, p. 22):
    When I thy singing next shall hear,
    I'll wish I might turn all to ear.
Perhaps an echo of *Carm.* xiii, 13-14, quoted in (12).

(5)   *To Anthea* (Moorman, p. 24):
    Ah, my Anthea! Must my heart still break?
    (*Love makes me write, what shame forbids to speak.*)
    Give me a kiss, and to that kiss a score;
    Then to that twenty, add an hundred more:
    A thousand to that hundred: so kiss on,
    To make that thousand up a million.
    Treble that million, and when that is done,
    Let's kiss afresh, as when we first begun.
    But yet, though Love likes well such scenes as these,
    There is an act that will more fully please:
    Kissing and glancing, soothing, all make way
    But to the acting of this private play:
    Name it I would; but being blushing red,
    The rest I'll speak, when we meet both in bed.
The second line is from Ovid's *Heroides, Phaedra to Hippolytus:*
    Dicere quae puduit scribere iussit amor;
the succeeding six are clearly inspired by the often quoted *Carm.* v:
    Da mi basia mille, deinde centum,
    Dein mille altera, dein secunda centum.
It is interesting to note how, in the latter part of the poem, Herrick turns from his
Latin sources to an original coarseness, distinctly his own.

(6)   From *To the Reverend Shade of his Religious Father* (Moorman, p. 27):
    That for seven lusters I did never come
    To do the rites to thy religious tomb:
    That neither hair was cut, nor true tears shed
    By me, o'r thee, (*as justments to the dead*)
    Forgive, forgive me; since I did not know
    Whether thy bones had here their rest, or no.
    But now 'tis known, behold; behold, I bring
    Unto thy ghost, th' effusèd offering:
    And look, what smallage, night-shade, cypress, yew,
    Unto the shades have been, or now are due,
    Here I devote. . . . .

These lovely verses are plainly influenced by Catullus's superlatively pathetic farewell at the tomb of his brother (*Carm.* ci):

> Multas per gentes et multa per aequora vectus
>   Advenio has miseras, frater, ad inferias,
> Ut te postremo donarem munere mortis
>   Et mutam nequiquam adloquerer cinerem,
> Quandoquidem fortuna mihi tete abstulit ipsum,
>   Heu miser indigne frater adempte mihi.
> Nunc tamen interea haec, prisco quae more parentum
>   Tradita sunt tristi munere ad inferias,
> Accipe fraterno multum manantia fletu
>   Atque in perpetuum, frater, ave atque vale.

(7) From *An Epitaph upon a Sober Matron* (Moorman, p. 41):

> My modest wedlock, that was known
> Contented with the bed of one.

See *Carm.* cxi, 1-2:

> Aufilena, viro contentam vivere solo
>   Nuptarum laus e laudibus eximiis.

(8) *An Epithalamie to Sir Thomas Southwell and his Lady* (Moorman, pp. 53-58) is full of references to the Catullian epithalamia.

(a) The frequently recurring refrain:

> Then away; come, Hymen, guide
> To the bed the bashful bride,

is very like the often repeated invocation of *Carm.* lxii:

> Hymen o Hymenaee, Hymen ades o Hymenaee,

and echoes also *Carm.* lxi, 31-32:

> Ac domum dominam voca
> Coniugis cupidam novi.

(b) Is it (sweet maid) your fault these holy
     Bridal-rites go on so slowly?

See *Carm.* lxi, 94-95:

> Sed moraris, abit dies:
> Prodeas, nova nupta.

(c) These precious-pearly-purling tears,
     But spring from ceremonious fears.
       And 'tis but native shame,
       That hides the loving flame.

See *Carm.* lxi, 83-86:

> Tardet ingenuus pudor:
> Quem tamen magis audiens
> Flet quod ire necesse est.
> Flere desine.

(d) And now the yellow veil, at last,
     Over her fragrant cheek is cast.

See *Carm.* lxi, 8-9:

> Flammeum cape, laetus huc,
> Huc veni. . .

(e) You, you that be of her nearest kin,
Now o'er the threshold force her in.

See *Carm.* lxi, 166-168:

> Transfer omine cum bono
> Limen aureolos pedes,
> Rasilemque subi forem.

(f) O Venus! thou, to whom is known
The best way how to loose the zone
   Of virgins!

See *Carm.* lxi, 52-53:

>   Tibi virgines
> Zonula solvunt sinus.

(g) But all fair signs appear
Within the chamber here.

See Latin quotation, *omine cum bono*, in (e) above.

(h) Virgins, weep not; 'twill come, when,
As she, so you'll be ripe for men.

See *Carm.* lxi, 36-38:

> Vosque item simul, integrae
> Virgines, quibus advenit
> Par dies.

(i) Now bar the doors, the bride-groom puts
The eager boys to gather nuts.

See *Carm.* lxi, 128:

> Nec nuces pueris neget.

(j) With all lucky birds to side
With the bride-groom, and the bride.

See *Carm.* lxi, 19-20:

> —Bona cum bona
> Nubet alite virgo.

(9) From *Corinna's Going a Maying* (Moorman, p. 69):

> Our life is short; and our days run
> As fast away as does the sun:
> And as a vapour or a drop of rain
> Once lost, can ne'er be found again:
> So when or you or I are made
> A fable, song, or fleeting shade;
> All love, all liking, all delight
> Lies drown'd with us in endless night.

Herrick has unquestionably in mind the familiar lines of *Carm.* v:

Soles occidere et redire possunt,
Nobis, sum semel occidit brevis lux,
Nox est perpetua una dormienda.

(10)   From *An Ode to Master Endymion Porter, upon His Brother's Death* (Moorman, p. 72):

Days may conclude in nights; and suns may rest,
   As dead, within the West;
Yet the next morn, re-gild the fragrant East.

Alas for me! that I have lost
   E'en all almost:
Sunk is my light; set is my sun;
And all the loom of life undone.

See the quotation from *Carm.* v. in (9).

(11)   From *The Welcome to Sack* (Moorman, p. 77):

So meet stolen kisses, when the moony nights
Call forth fierce lovers to their wish'd delights.

Perhaps an echo of *Carm.* vii:

Basiationes. . . .
. . .Quam sidera multa, cum tacet nox,
Furtivos hominum vident amores.

(12)   From *To Live Merrily, and to Trust to Good Verses* (Moorman, p. 80):

A goblet next I'll drink
   To Ovid; and suppose,
Made he the pledge, he'd think
   The world had all one nose.

See *Carm.* xiii, 13-14:

Quod tu cum olfacies, deos rogabis
Totum ut te faciant, Fabulle, nasum.

(13)   *Ibid.:*

Then this immensive cup
   Of aromatic wine,
Catullus, I quaff up
   To that terse Muse of thine.

Here Catullus figures as one of a most honorable group: Homer, Vergil, Ovid, Propertius, and Tibullus are the other poets commemorated.

(14)   From *Lips Tongueless* (Moorman, p. 82):

For my part, I never care
For those lips that tongue-tied are;
Tell-tales I would have them be
Of my Mistress, and of me.

For a parallel sentiment, see *Carm.* lv, 18-20:

Si linguam clauso tenes in ore,
Fructus proicies amoris omnes:
Verbosa gaudet Venus loquella.

(15)   From *To His Friend, on the Untuneable Times* (Moorman, p. 84):
>   Play I could once; but (gentle friend) you see
>   My harp hung up, here on the willow-tree.
>   Sing I could once; and bravely too inspire
>   (With luscious numbers) my melodious lyre. . .
>   Grief (my dear friend) has first my harp unstrung;
>   Wither'd my hand, and palsy-struck my tongue.

Herrick, in all probability, had in mind *Carm.* lxviii, 13-14, 19-20, 25-26:
>   Accipe quis merser fortunae fluctibus ipse,
>   Ne amplius a misero dona beata petas. . .
>   Sed totum hoc studium luctu fraterna mihi mors
>   Abstulit. . . .
>   Cuius ego interitu tota de mente fugavi
>   Haec studia atque omnes delicias animi.

(16)   From *The Plaudite, or End of Life* (Moorman, p. 94):
>   If after rude and boist'rous seas,
>   My wearied pinnace here finds ease;
>   If so be I've gain'd the shore
>   With safety of a faithful oar:
>   If having run my bark on ground,
>   Ye see the aged vessel crown'd. . . .

Here Herrick seems to have in mind Catullus's dedication of his pinnace, *Carm.* iv:
>   Phasellus ille, quem videtis, hospites,
>   . . . Dicit . . .
>   Tuo imbuisse palmulas in aequore,
>   Et inde tot per impotentia freta
>   Erum tulisse. . .
>   . . . Cum veniret a mari
>   Novissimo hunc ad usque limpidum lacum.
>   Sed haec prius fuere: nunc recondita
>   Senet quiete seque dedicat tibi,
>   Gemelle Castor et gemelle Castoris.

(17)   From *Not to Love* (Moorman, p. 102):
>   There be in love as many fears
>   As the summer's corn has ears:
>   Sighs, and sobs, and sorrows more
>   Than the sand that makes the shore.

For the first simile Herrick apparently has in mind *Carm.* xlviii, 5-6:
>   Non si densior aridis aristis
>   Sit nostrae seges osculationis.

For a parallel to the second couplet, see *Carm.* vii, 3:
>   Quam magnus numerus Libyssae harenae. . .

(18)   From *Upon the Death of His Sparrow, An Elegy* (Moorman, pp. 103-104):
>   Phil, the late dead, the late dead dear,

O! may no eye distill a tear
For you once lost, who weep not here!
Had Lesbia (too-too kind) but known
This sparrow, she had scorn'd her own:
And for this dead which under-lies,
Wept out our heart, as well as eyes.
But, endless Peace, sit here and keep
My Phil, the time he has to sleep. . . .

An elegant little elaboration of the famous *Carm.* iii:

Lugete, O Veneres Cupidinesque,
Et quantum est hominum venustiorum!
Passer mortuus est meae puellae. . . . .

(19)   From *To Anthea, Who May Command Him Anything* (Moorman, p. 109):

Thou art my life, my love, my heart,
The very eyes of me.

This may be an echo of *Carm.* lxxxii:

Quinti, si tibi vis oculos debere Catullum
Aut aliud si quid carius est oculis,
Eripere ei noli multo quod carius illi
Est oculis seu quid carius est oculis.

(20)   From *A Nuptial Song, or Epithalamy, on Sir Clipseby Crew and His Lady* (Moorman, pp. 112-116):

Hymen, O Hymen! tread the sacred ground;
Shew thy white feet, and head with marjoram crown'd:
Mount up thy flames, and let thy torch
Display the bridegroom in the porch. . .

See *Carm.* lxi, 6-10, 14-15:

Cinge tempora floribus
Suave olentis amaraci,
Flammeum cape, laetus huc,
Huc veni niveo gerens
Luteum pede soccum. . .
Pelle humum pedibus, manu
Pineam quate taedam.

There are further traces of Catullus in this poem, but they are so altered and transmuted into seventeenth century terms that they would not repay quotation.

(21)   *Upon Shark, Epig.* (Moorman, p. 118):

Shark, when he goes to any public feast,
Eats to one's thinking, of all there, the least.
What saves the master of the house thereby?
When if the servants search they may descry
In his wide codpiece, (dinner being done)
Two napkins cramm'd up, and a silver spoon.

See *Carm.* xii, 1-3:

> Marrucine Asini, manu sinistra
> Non belle uteris in ioco atque vino:
> Tollis lintea negligentiorum. . .

(22) *Casualties* (Moorman, p. 123):

> Good things, that come of course, far less do please,
> Than those which come by sweet contingencies.

See *Carm.* cvii, 1-2:

> Si cui quid cupido optantique obtigit unquam
>   Insperanti, hoc est gratum animo proprie.

(23) *On Himself* (Moorman, p. 131):

> Ask me, why I do not sing
> To the tension of the string,
> As I did, not long ago,
> When my numbers full did flow?
> Grief (ay me!) hath struck my lute,
> And my tongue at one time mute.

See *Carm.* lxviii, quoted in (15).

(24) From *His Age, Dedicated to His Peculiar Friend, M. John Wickes,* under *the name of Posthumus* (Moorman, p. 133):

> —We see the seas
>   And moons to wane;
> But they fill up their ebbs again:
>   But vanish'd man,
> Like to a lily-lost, ne'er can. . . .

See, for a parallel passage, *Carm.* v, quoted in (9).

(25) *Ibid.*:

> — And mark each one
> Day with the white and lucky stone.

See *Carm.* lxviii, 148:

> Quem lapide illa diem candidiore notat.

(26) From *A Canticle to Apollo* (Moorman, p. 151):

> Hark, hark, the god does play!
> And as he leads the way
> Through heaven, the very spheres,
> As men, turn all to ears.

For a parallel passage see *Carm.* xiii, 13-14, quoted in (12).

(27) From *To His Book* (Moorman, p. 155):

> Have I not blest thee? Then go forth; nor fear
> Or spice, or fish, or close-stools here. . . .

ee *Carm.* xcv, 8, quoted in (37), where the reference is more explicit and clear.

(28)   From *How He Would Drink His Wine* (Moorman, p. 187):
>   Fill me my wine in crystal; thus, and thus
>   I'd see't in's *puris naturalibus:*
>   Unmixt. I love to have it smirk and shine;
>   *'Tis sin I know, 'tis sin to throttle wine.*

This is possibly influenced by *Carm.* xxvii, 5-7:
>   At vos quo libet hinc abite, lymphae,
>   Vini pernicies, et ad severos
>   Migrate; hic merus est Thyonianus;

but the last line is in Martial, I, 19: *Scelus est iugulare Falernum.*

(29)   From *To His Worthy Kinsman, Mr. Stephen Soame* (Moorman, p. 199):
>   Among which holies, be thou ever known,
>   Brave kinsman, markt out with the whiter stone.

For "whiter stone" see *Carm.* lxviii, 148, quoted in (25) above.

(30)   From *An Apparition of His Mistress Calling him to Elysium* (Moorman, p. 206):
>   Then soft Catullus, sharp-fang'd Martial,
>   And tow'ring Lucan, Horace, Juvenal. . .
>   —Thou shalt there
>   Behold them in a spacious theater.

The epithet "soft" is an unusual one to apply to Catullus; Herrick probably has in mind Catullus's description of his own verses in *Carm.* xvi, 3-4:
>   Qui me ex versiculis meis putastis,
>   Quod sunt *molliculi*, parum pudicum. . .

(31)   From *A Nuptial Verse to Mistress Elizabeth Lee, Now Lady Tracy* (Moorman, p. 216):
>   The field is pitch'd; but such must be your wars
>   As that your kisses must out-vie the stars.

For the familiar simile of likening the kisses of the transports of love to the number of stars, see *Carm.* vii, 7:
>   [Basiationes] quam sidera multa, cum tacet nox.

(32)   *Poets* (Moorman, p. 218):
>   Wantons we are; and though our words be such,
>   Our lives do differ from our lines by much.

See Catullus's disclaimer of an evil life, *Carm.* xvi, 5-6:
>   Nam castum esse decet pium poetam
>   Ipsum, versiculos nihil necesse est.

(33)   *To Sappho* (Moorman, p. 238):
>   Let us now take time, and play,
>   Love, and live here while we may;
>   Drink rich wine; and make good cheer,
>   While we have our being here:
>   For, once dead, and laid i'th grave,
>   No return from thence we have.

Here Herrick clearly has in mind the theme of the *Vivamus, mea Lesbia, atque amemus, Carm.* v.

(34) From *His Return to London* (Moorman, p. 242):
    From the dull confines of the drooping West,
    To see the day spring from the pregnant East,
    Ravish'd in spirit, I come, nay more, I fly
    To thee, blest place of my nativity!
    Thus, thus with hallowed feet I touch the ground,
    With thousand blessings by thy fortune crown'd. . .

Herrick seems to have at the back of his mind Catullus's verses on his return to Sirmio, *Carm.* xxxi, 4-9:
    Quam te libenter quamque laetus inviso,
    Vix mi ipse credens Thyniam atque Bithynos
    Liquisse campos et videre te in tuto!
    O quid solutis est beatius curis,
    Cum mens onus reponit, ac peregrino
    Labore fessi venimus larem ad nostrum
    Desideratoque adquiescimus lecto?

(35) *Our Own Sins Unseen* (Moorman, p. 253):
    Other men's sins we ever bear in mind;
    None sees the fardel of his faults behind.

See *Carm.* xxii, 20-21:
    . . . Suus cuique attributus est error,
    Sed non videmus manticae quod in tergo est.

Pollard suggests (II, p. 284) Seneca, *De Ira*, ii, 28: *Aliena vitia in oculis habemus; a tergo nostra sunt.* Catullus, however, is the more likely source.

(36) *No Pains, No Gains* (Moorman, p. 253):
    If little labor, little are our gains:
    Man's fortunes are according to his pains.

Perhaps an echo of *Carm.* lxii, 16:
    Iure igitur vincemur; amat victoria curam.

(37) *To His Book* (Moorman, p. 275):
    Make haste away, and let one be
    A friendly patron unto thee:
    Lest rapt from hence, I see thee lie
    Torn for the use of pasterie:
    Or see thy injur'd leaves serve well
    To make loose gowns for mackerel:
    Or see the grocers in a trice
    Make hoods of thee to serve out spice.

For the italicized couplet see *Carm.* xcv, 7-8:
    At Volusi annales Paduam morientur ad ipsam
      Et laxas scombris saepe dabunt tunicas.

(38)   *To Sappho* (Moorman, p. 279):
> Thou says't thou lov'st me, Sappho; I say no;
> But would to Love I could believe 'twas so!
> Pardon my fears (sweet Sappho); I desire
> That thou be righteous found: and I the liar.

This is in the very mood of *Carm.* cix:
> Iucundum, mea vita, mihi proponis amorem
>   Hunc nostrum inter nos perpetuumque fore.
> Di magni, facite ut vere promittere possit
>   Atque id sincere dicat et ex animo.

(39)   From *A Request to the Graces* (Moorman, p. 290):
> *Numbers ne'er tickle, or but lightly please,*
> *Unless they have some wanton carriages.*

The immediate source is undoubtedly, as Pollard points out (II, 290), Martial, I, xxxvi:
> Lex haec carminibus data est jocosis,
> Ne possint, nisi pruriant, iuvare;

but Martial had unquestionably in mind *Carm.* xvi, 8-9:
>   . . . Versiculos . . .
> Si sunt molliculi ac parum pudici
> Et quod pruriat incitare possunt.

(40)   *Upon Bliss* (Moorman, p. 295):
> Bliss (last night drunk) did kiss his mother's knee:
> Where he will kiss (next drunk) conjecture ye.

For such vulgarity Herrick has unfortunately too much precedent in Catullus. See, for one example, *Carm.* lxxxix, 1-2:
> Gellius est tenuis: quid ni? cui tam bona mater
>   Tamque valens vivat tamque venusta soror. . .

(41)   Concluding couplet (Moorman, p. 335):
> To his book's end this last line he'd have plac't,
> *Jocund his Muse was; but his Life was chaste.*

Moorman points out that this is a quotation from Ovid, *Tristia*, ii, 354:
> Vita verecunda est, musa iocosa, mihi.[9]

But Ovid is here borrowing from Catullus, *Carm.* xvi, 5-6, for which see (32).

(42)   From *A Carol Presented to Dr. Williams, Bishop of Lincoln, as a New-Year's Gift* (Moorman, p. 413):
> But all we wither and our light
> Is spilt in everlasting night.
> When as your sight
> Shows like the heavens above the moon,
> Like an eternal noon
> That sees no setting sun.

Herrick unquestionably has in mind here the famous lines in *Carm.* v, *Soles occidere et redire possunt*, for which see (9).

9 Moorman, *op. cit.*, p. 120.

JOHN MILTON
(1608-1674)

The traces of Catullus in the poetry of Milton are so few and slight as to be well nigh negligible. That Milton knew Catullus is fairly certain; were there no direct reference made to the Latin poet the probabilities would still be that Milton, omnivorous reader of the classics that we know him to have been, was acquainted with him. But Milton refers specifically to Catullus in a way which shows he thought himself competent to pass judgment upon Catullus's style: "Nor was the satirical sharpness, or naked plainness of Lucilius, or Catullus, or Flaccus, by any order prohibited."[1] But in all his lyrical verse there is but one possible reference to Catullus, and that is a doubtful one.

(1)   From *L'Allegro*, 125:
      There let Hymen oft appear
      In saffron robe, with taper clear.

For "saffron robe" see *Carm*. lxi, 8, "Flammeun cape," and the "taper clear" finds its counterpart in lxi, 15, "Pineam quate taedam." But these are stock terms in describing Hymen; see, for example, (1) in FLETCHER.

Turning now from the lyrical poems, there are, so far as I can discover, three possible references to Catullus in Milton's longer poems.

(2) In *Paradise Lost*, II, ll. 900-905:
                  They around the flag. . . .
      Swarm populous, unnumbered as the sands
      Of Barca or Cyrene's torrid soil,
      Levied to side with warring winds.
See *Carm*. vii, 3-4:
      Quam magnus numerus Libyssae harenae
      Laserpiciferis iacet Cyrenis.

(3)   In *Paradise Lost*, V, ll. 215-219:
                  They led the vine
      To wed her elm; she, spoused, about him twines
      Her marriageable arms, and with her brings
      Her dower, the adopted clusters, to adorn
      His barren leaves.
This seems almost certainly an echo of *Carm*. lxii, 49-54:
      Ut vidua in nudo vitis quae nascitur arvo. . .
      . . . Si forte eadem est ulmo coniuncta marito. . .

(4)   In *Samson Agonistes*, ll. 131-133:
            Useless the forgery
      Of brazen shield and spear, the hammered cuirass,
      Chalybean-tempered steel. . . .
There is in Catullus a parallel allusion, *Carm*. lxvi, 48-50:
      Iuppiter, ut Chalybon omne genus pereat,
      Et qui principio sub terra quaerere venas
      Institit ac ferri stringere duritiem!

---

1   Milton, *Areopagitica*, in Arber's English Reprints, p. 38.

ANDREW MARVELL
(1621-1678)

Marvell's classical erudition was not great; as Professor Grierson whimsically says, this young friend of Milton's "imbibed no more of Milton's classical inspiration than his graceless nephews and pupils, the Phillipses."[1] In his greatest love poem, indeed, he attained a lofty and vehement sincerity, which Mr. T. S. Eliot justly feels to be comparable with the fiery earnestness of Catullus, though he denies to it "the grand reverberation" of the *Vivamus, mea Lesbia.*[2] The poem is, of course, the magnificent apostrophe *To His Coy Mistress:*

> But at my back I always hear
> Time's wingèd chariot hurrying near,
> And yonder all before us lie
> Deserts of vast eternity.
> Thy beauty shall no more be found,
> Nor, in thy marble vault, shall sound
> My echoing song; then worms shall try
> That long preserved virginity,
> And your quaint honor turn to dust
> And into ashes all my lust:
> The grave's a fine and private place
> But none, I think, do there embrace.

These lines are worthy of Catullus, surely, and reminiscent of his passionate yet tender sincerity, but, though Marvell may have on occasion some of the spirit of Catullus, the traces of any direct Catullian influence in his poems are slight, and, frankly, uncertain.

(1) From *To His Coy Mistress:*
> Thus, though we can not make our sun
> Stand still, yet we will make him run.

A possible reference to the famous *Soles occidere et redire possunt* of *Carm.* v.

(2) From *On the Death of the Lord Hastings:*
> Only they drooping Hymeneus note,
> Who for sad purple tears his saffron-coat,
> And trails his torches through the starry hall,
> Reversèd at his darling's funeral.

See the often-quoted description of Hymen, lxi, 6-15.

(3) From *A Poem upon the Death of his Late Highness The Lord Protector:*
> He without noise still travelled to his end,
> As silent suns to meet the night descend.

It is barely possible that this may be an echo of the passage in *Carm.* v, mentioned in (1).

1 Grierson, *The Background of English Literature*, p. 155.
2 W. H. Bagguley, *Andrew Marvell, Tercentenary Tributes*, p. 67.

ABRAHAM COWLEY
(1618-1667)

There is very little of the high lyric strain in Cowley; he is a polished and versatile maker of verses, ingenious, subtle, and learned, but with little of the true poetic fire. His love poems, in which we should look especially for the influence of Catullus, are hopelessly cold and artificial, utterly unlike Catullus's bursts of lyric passion. "The compositions," says Johnson, "are such as might have been written for penance by a hermit, or for hire by a philosophical rhymer who had only heard of another sex."[1] In his poems, as in those of Waller, there is evident the dawning of the Augustan age; even those lovely verses in which he condones the apostasy of his dear friend Crashaw to the Roman church have more of the spirit of Pope than of the early Jacobeans or Carolinians:

> Pardon, my Mother Church, if I consent
> That angels led him when from thee he went,
> For even in error sure no danger is
> When join'd with so much piety as his.
> Ah, mighty God, with shame I speak't, and grief,
> Ah, that our greatest faults were in belief!. . .
> His Faith perhaps in some nice tenents might
> Be wrong; his Life, I'm sure, was in the right.[2]

Cowley's verse is at its worst frigid and deadeningly intellectual; at its best it does not rise much above the graceful and the serenely thoughtful. "Judged by the accepted tests of great poetry," says Mr. Sparrow, "high seriousness, passion, emotion recollected, though much of it must be found wanting, there is much that remains."[3] That "much" must be found, if found at all, in the shorter poems of *The Mistress*; the *Davideis* and the *Pindaric Odes* come, in the main, close to being dreary wastes of words. I have, in this study, made use not only of Cowley's lyrics in *The Mistress*, but of his longer poems and the verses included in the prose works; his knowledge of Catullus is large, and the skill with which he made use of his borrowings, noteworthy. Cowley's translation of the *Acme and Septimius* of Catullus I shall have occasion to speak of later; it is a graceful translation of a charming little poem, otherwise neglected by the poets of the century.

(1)   From *Leaving Me and Then Loving Many* (Waller, p. 79):
> — Since my Love his vanquisht world forsook,
> Murther'd by poisons from her falsehood took,
> An hundred petty kings claim each their part,
> And rend that glorious empire of her heart.

This is reminiscent of *Carm.* xi, and especially of 17-18, and 21:
> Cum suis vivat valeatque moechis,
> Quos simul complexa tenet trecentos. . .
> Nec meum respectet, ut ante, amorem.

---

1   Johnson, *Lives of the Poets: Cowley.*
2   *On the Death of Mr. Crashaw* (Waller, p. 49).
3   John Sparrow, *The Mistress*, p. xix.

(2)   From *The Heart Fled Again* (Waller, p. 105):
> The doleful Ariadne so,
>> On the wide shore forsaken stood:
> False Theseus, whither dost thou go?
>> Afar false Theseus cut the flood.
>> But Bacchus came to her relief. . .

This is plainly inspired by the incident of Ariadne in *Carm.* lxiv; see especially 57-59:
> Desertam in sola miseram se cernat harena.
> Immemor at iuvenis fugiens pellit vada remis,
> Irrita ventosae linquens promissa procellae;

and 251-253:
> At parte ex alia florens volitabat Iacchus. . .
> Te quaerens, Ariadna, tuoque incensus amore.

(3)   From the poem beginning *Then Like Some Wealthy Island Thou Shalt Lie* (Waller, pp. 114-115):
> Yet nothing, but the Night our sports shall know;
>> Night that's both blind and silent too.
>
> . . . .
>
> Men, out of wisdom; women, out of pride,
>> The pleasant thefts of Love do hide.

See *Carm.* lxviii, 145-146:
> Sed furtiva dedit mira munuscula nocte
>> Ipsius ex ipso dempta viri gremio.

(4)   From *The Encrease* (Waller, p. 122):
> I thought, I'll swear, I could have lov'd no more
>> Than I had done before;
>> But you as easi'ly might account
> Till to the top of numbers you amount,
>> As cast up my Love's score.
> Ten thousand millions was the sum;
> Millions of endless millions are to come.

For this device of casting up a formal reckoning of loves (or kisses) see the familiar *Carm.* v, 7-13.

(5)   From *The Dissembler* (Waller, p. 133):
> My lines of amorous desire
> I wrote to kindle and blow others' fire.

See, for the function which Catullus assigns to his lyrics, *Carm.* xvi, 6-11:
> —Versiculos—
> Qui tum denique habent salem ac leporem,
> Si sunt molliculi ac parum pudici
> Et quod pruriat incitare possunt,
> Non dico pueris, sed his pilosis,
> Qui duros nequeunt movere lumbos.

(6)   From *Love Given Over* (Waller, p. 151):
        It is enough; enough of time, and pain
        Hast thou consum'd in vain;
        Leave, wretched Cowley, leave
        Thyself with shadows to deceive;
    Count that already lost which thou must never gain.

        . . . .
        Resolve then on it, and by force or art
        Free thy unlucky heart.

Clearly inspired by *Carm.* viii:
        Miser Catulle, desinas ineptire,
        Et quod vides perisse perditum ducas. . .
        Nunc iam illa non vult: tu quoque, impotens, noli,
        Nec quae fugit sectare, nec miser vive,
        Sed obstinata mente perfer, obdura.

(7)   *Ode*: *Acme and Septimius, out of Catullus* (Waller, p. 419):

        Whilst on Septimius' panting breast
        (Meaning nothing less than rest)
        Acme lean'd her loving head,
        Thus the pleas'd Septimius said:

        My dearest Acme, if I be
        Once alive, and love not thee,
        With a passion far above
        All that e'er was called Love,
        In a Lybian desert may
        I become some lion's prey;
        Let him, Acme, let him tear
        My breast—when Acme is not there.

        The God of Love, who stood to hear him,
        (The God of Love was always near him)
        Pleas'd and tickl'd with the sound,
        Sneez'd aloud; and all around
        The little Loves that waited by,
        Bow'd and bless'd the augury.

        Acme, enflam'd with what he said,
        Rear'd her gently-bending head,
        And her purple mouth with joy
        Stretching to the delicious boy,
        Twice (and twice could scarce suffice)
        She kiss'd his drunken, rolling eyes.

My little Life, my All (said she)
So may we ever servants be
To this best God, and ne'er retain
Our hated liberty again;
So may thy passion last for me,
As I a passion have for thee,
Greater and fiercer much than can
Be conceiv'd by thee, a man.
Into my marrow is it gone,
Fix'd and settled in the bone,
It reigns not only in my heart,
But runs, like life, through ev'ry part.

She spoke; the God of Love aloud
Sneez'd again, and all the crowd
Of little Loves that waited by,
Bow'd, and bless'd the augury.

This good omen, thus from Heaven,
Like a happy signal given,
Their Loves and Lives (all four) embrace,
And hand in hand run all the race.
To poor Septimius (who did now
Nothing else but Acme grow)
Acme's bosom was alone
The whole world's imperial throne,
And to faithful Acme's mind
Septimius was all human kind.

If the Gods would please to be
But advis'd for once by me,
I'd advise 'em, when they spy
Any illustrious piety,
To reward her, if it be she,
To reward him, if it be he,
With such a husband, such a wife,
With Acme's and Septimius' life.

A delightful paraphrase of a delightful little poem, *Carm.* xlv. Cowley showed rare taste in his choice of a poem for translation; the Latin poem is practically ignored by other poets of the period. The concluding stanza is wholly Cowley's:

Acmen Septimius suos amores
Tenens in gremio 'Mea' inquit, 'Acme,
Ni te perdite amo atque amare porro
Omnes sum adsidue paratus annos

Quantum qui pote plurimum perire,
Solus in Libya Indiaque tosta
Caesio veniam obvius leoni.'
Hoc ut dixit, Amor, sinistra ut ante,
Dextram sternuit adprobationem.
At Acme leviter caput reflectens
Et dulcis pueri ebrios ocellos
Illo purpureo ore saviata,
'Sic,' inquit, 'mea vita, Septimille,
Huic uni domino usque serviamus,
Ut multo mihi maior acriorque
Ignis mollibus ardet in medullis.'
Hoc ut dixit, Amor, sinistra ut ante,
Dextram sternuit adprobationem.
Nunc ab auspicio bono profecti
Mutuis animis amant amantur.
Unam Septimius misellus Acmen
Mavult quam Syrias Britanniasque:
Uno in Septimio fidelis Acme
Facit delicias libidinesque.
Quis ullos homines beatiores
Vidit, quis Venerem auspicatiorem?

There are several references to Catullus in Cowley's other works, which, though lying outside our consideration of Catullus's influence on lyric poetry, we may include for completeness.

(8)   In his metaphrase of *The Second Olympic Ode of Pindar* (Waller, p. 158), in his note explanatory of the lines:

They Agrigentum built, the beauteous eye
    Of fair-face'd Sicily,

he writes (Waller, p. 164):

So Julian terms Damascus, τῆς ἑώας ἁπάσης ὀφθαλμὸν, the eye of all the East. So Catullus, Sirmium, *insularum ocellum*, the eye of islands.

See *Carm.* xxxi, 1-2:

Paene insularum, Sirmio, insularumque
Ocelle.

(9)   In explanation of a passage in the *Davideis*, II (Waller, p. 290):

Ten pieces of bright tapestry hung the room,
The noblest work e'er stretch'd on Syrian loom,

he sets forth in his notes (Waller, p. 308) that:

The custom of having stories wrought in hangings, coverlets, nay even wearing garments, is made to be very ancient by the poets. Such is the history of Theseus and Ariadne in the coverlet of Thetis' *pulvinar*, or marriage bed. Catull. *Argonaut:*

> Talibus amplifice vestis variata figuris
> Pulvinar complexa suo velabat amictu.

Here he is quoting *Carm.* lxiv, 265-266.

(10)   In a note to the *Davideis*, I, he says (Waller, p. 274):

> That the Corybantes and effeminate priests of Cybele could be animated by it [music] to cut their own flesh. . . . is well known to all men conversant among authors.

He may well have in mind, specifically, Attis's sacrifice of his virility, *Carm.* lxiii, 4-5:

> Stimulatus ibi furenti rabie, vagus animis,
> Devoluit ili acuto sibi pondera silice.

(11)   Among his *Essays* he quotes and translates a short epigram of Catullus (*Carm.* lxxxv):

> "And yet our dear self is so wearisome to us that we can scarcely support its conversation for an hour together. This is such an odd temper of mind as Catullus expresses toward one of his mistresses, whom we may suppose to have been of a very unsociable humour.

> Odi et amo, quanam id faciam ratione requiris?
>   Nescio, sed fieri sentio, et excrucior.

> I hate, and yet I love thee too;
> How can that be? I know not how;
> Only that it is so I know,
> And feel with torment that 'tis so.[4]

Apparently Cowley knew his Catullus well enough to venture to quote from memory, for he badly misquotes the first line —

> . . . Quare id faciam fortasse requiris.

---

4 Waller, *Essays and Plays of Abraham Cowley*, p. 393.

SIR EDWARD SHERBURNE
(1618-1702)

Sherburne's inspiration is not primarily classical but French and Italian. His poems, to be sure, contain a number of translations from the Latin, but, with him as with so many of his contemporaries, the tinsel of Ausonius and Claudian weighed more heavily than the true gold of the Latin authors of the great age. The influence of Catullus upon Sherburne is not great; the two quotations which follow are references to some of the most familiar of the lines of Catullus, lines which had become, as it were, part of the poetical stock in trade, which he might well have come upon without having any direct knowledge of the Latin poet at all.

(1)   From *Love's Arithmetic* (Chalmers, VI, p. 627):

> By a gentle river laid
> Thirsis to his Phillis said:
> *Equal to these sandy grains*
> *Are the number of my pains:*
> And the drops within their bounds
> Speak the sum of all my wounds.
>
> Phillis, whom like passion burns,
> Thirsis answer thus returns:
> "Many, as the Earth hath leaves,
> Are the griefs my heart receives;
> *And the stars, which Heaven inspires,*
> *Reckon my consuming fires"*. . .
>
> "We will count our griefs with blisses,
> Thousand torments, thousand kisses."

The inspiration here seems to be Catullus's great "kissing poems," quoted often before, especially *Carm.* v. and *Carm.* vii.

(2)   From *The Broken Faith* (Chalmers, VI, p. 630):
> Ah false nymph! those words were fit
> In sand only to be writ:
> For the quickly rising streams
> Of oblivion, and the Thames,
> In a little moment's stay
> From the shore wash'd clear away
> What thy hand had there impress'd,
> And Myrtillo from thy breast.

Possibly suggested by *Carm.* lxx, 3-4:
> . . . Sed mulier cupido quod dicit amanti
>   In vento et rapida scribere oportet aqua.

EDMUND WALLER
(1606-1687)

Much of the work of the frigid and time-serving Waller, who rhymed insipidly under both Jameses, both Charleses, and the Protector, lies without the field of this study. I have dealt with all his verse, however, for the sake of completeness. Perhaps none of the men considered in these studies had less of the truly poetic and lyric than he; in him the Augustan age definitely begins and begins indifferently. He is a thoroughly bad poet. His love-verse is cold, artificial, and absurd:

> But, Celia, if you apprehend
> The muse of your incensed friend,
> Nor would that he recall your blame
> And make it live, repeat the same;
> Again deceive him, and again,
> And then he swears he'll not complain;
> For still to be deluded so,
> Is all the pleasure lovers know;
> Who, like good falconers, take delight,
> Not in the quarry, but the flight.[1]

As a courtier he is false and ridiculous; take, for example, his lines on the profligate Charles:

> On which reflecting in his mighty mind,
> No private passion does indulgence find;
> The pleasures of his youth suspended are,
> And made a sacrifice to public care.[2]

His judgment in literary matters is typical of the man:

> Though poets may of inspiration boast,
> Their rage, ill-governed, in the clouds is lost.
> He that proportioned wonders can disclose,
> At once his fancy and his judgment shows.
> Chaste moral writing we may learn from hence,
> Neglect of which no wit can recompense.[3]

But perhaps the essential tinsel of the man, his arrogant scorn of finer letters, show themselves most clearly in certain of his lines on Creech's translation of Lucretius:

> But let not this disturb thy tuneful head;
> Thou writ'st for thy delight, and not for bread;
> Thou art not cursed to write thy verse with care;
> But art above what other poets fear.[4]

The classical element in Waller is large, but his references are of the most conventional kind. I have been able to find few traces of any possible Catullian influence among his poems; Catullus he would probably not have approved of; he would think

---

1   *The Poems of Edmund Waller*, edited by G. Thorn Drury, p. 108.
2   *Ibid.*, p. 172.
3   *Ibid.*, p. 214.
4   *Ibid.*, p. 219.

his "rage ill governed." The quotations which follow show no certain Catullian influence.

    (1)   From *In Answer to One Who Writ against a Fair Lady*, (Drury, p. 25):
        So shall thy rebel wit become her prize.
        Should thy iambics swell into a book,
        All were confuted with one radiant look.

For the use of "iambics" as a general term for "satire," see *Carm.* xl, 1-2:
        Quaenam te mala mens, miselle Ravide,
        Agit praecipitem in meos iambos?

    (2)   From *For Drinking of Healths* (Drury, p. 89):
        Deserted Ariadne, thus supplied,
        Did perjured Theseus' cruelty deride;
        Bacchus embraced, from her exalted thought
        Banished the man, her passion, and his fault.

This may show a perverted acquaintance with the Bacchus and Ariadne episode of *Carm.* lxiv.

    (3)   From *Epitaph to be Written under the Latin Inscription upon the Tomb of the Only Son of Lord Andover* (Drury, p. 191):
        His parents' pious care, their name, their joy,
        And all their hope, lies buried with this boy.

See *Carm.* lxviii, 22-23:
        Tecum una tota est nostra sepulta domus,
        Omnia tecum una perierunt gaudia nostra.

HENRY PEACHAM
(1576?-1643?)

SAMUEL SHEPPARD
(fl. 1646)

These very minor poets find a place here only as the authors of two epithalamia modeled very closely upon, indeed, translated in large part from, *Carm.* lxi of Catullus. The following poem by Henry Peacham is the third of a series of four *Nuptial Hymns in Honor of the Marriage* (between Frederick, Count Palatine of the Rhine, and the Princess Elizabeth), solemnized February 14, 1613. In this poem and in Sheppard's following, I use Case's text.[1]

The text follows—almost an exact translation of part of Catullus's *Carm.* lxi, save that a very few temporal allusions of the period are woven in:

> Urania's son, who dwell'st upon
> The fertile top of Helicon,
> Chaste marriage sovereign, and dost lead
> The virgin to her bridal bed:
>   Io, Hymen, Hymenaeus!
>
> With marjoram begirt thy brow,
> And take the veil of yellow: now
> Ye piny torches with your light,
> To golden day convert the night:
>   Io, Hymen, Hymenaeus!
>
> See how like the Cyprian queen,
> Eliza comes; as when (I ween)
> On Ida hill the prize she had
> Allotted by the Phygian lad:
>   Io, Hymen, Hymenaeus!
>
> As Asian myrtle fresh and fair,
> Which Hamadryads with their care,
> And duly tending by the floods,
> Have taught to over-look the woods:
>   Io, Hymen, Hymenaeus!
>
> Behold how Vesper from the sky
> Consenteth by his twinkling eye;
> And Cynthia stays her swans to see
> The state of this solemnity:
>   Io, Hymen, Hymenaeus!

---

1 Robert H. Case, *English Epithalamies*, p. 56.

Wedlock, were it not for thee,
We could not child nor parent see;
Armies, countries to defend,
Or shepherds, hilly herds to tend:
   Io, Hymen, Hymenaeus!

But, Hymen, call the nymph away,
With torches' light the children stay,
Whose sparks (see how!) ascend on high
As if there wanted stars in sky:
   Io, Hymen, Hymenaeus!

As virgin vine her elm doth wed,
His oak the ivy over-spread;
So chaste desires thou join'st in one,
That disunited were undone:
   Io, Hymen, Hymenaeus!

But see! her golden foot hath past
The doubled threshold, and at last
She doth approach her bridal-bed,
Of none save Tiber envyed:
   Io, Hymen, Hymenaeus!

Chaste marriage-bed, he sooner tells
The stars, the ocean sand, or shells,
That thinks to number those delights,
Wherewith thou short'nest longest nights:
   Io, Hymen, Hymenaeus!

With richest Tyrian purple spread,
Where her dear spouse is laid on bed,
Like young Ascanius, or the lad
Her love the queen of Cyprus had:
   Io, Hymen, Hymenaeus!

Young Frederick, of royal line,
Of Cassimires, who on the Rhine
To none are second said to be
For valour, bounty, piety:
   Io, Hymen, Hymenaeus!

Come bride-maid Venus, and undo
Th' Herculean knot with fingers two;
And take the girdle from her waist,
That virgins must forego at last:
    Io, Hymen, Hymenaeus!

Scatter nuts without the door,
The married is a child no more;
For whoso'er a wife hath wed
Hath other business in his head:
    Io, Hymen, Hymenaeus!

Where, pass ye many an happy night
Until Lucina brings to light
An hopeful prince, who may restore,
In part, the loss we had before:
    Io, Hymen, Hymenaeus!

That one day we may live to see
A Frederick Henry on her knee;
Who mought to Europe give her law,
And keep encroaching Hell in awe:
    Io, Hymen, Hymenaeus!

Upon whose brow may envy read
The reconcile of love and dread;
And in whose rosy cheek we see
His mother's graceful modesty:
    Io, Hymen, Hymenaeus!

But, Muse of mine, we but molest,
I doubt, with ruder song their rest:
The doors are shut, and light about
Extinct; then time thy flame were out:
    Io, Hymen, Hymenaeus!

Sheppard's poem, taken from the *Loves of Amandus and Sophronia*, is almost a translation of the first forty lines of *Carm.* lxi. Here, too, the text is Case's[2]:

Epithalamium.

Heavenly fair Urania's son,
Thou that dwell'st on Helicon,
Hymen, O thy brows impale,
To the bride the bridegroom hale.
Take thy saffron robe and come

With sweet-flowered marjoram;
Yellow socks of woollen wear,
With a smiling look appear;
Shrill Epithalamiums sing,
Let this day with pleasure spring;
Nimble dance; the flaming tree
Take in that fair hand of thine.
Let good auguries combine
For the pair that now are wed;
Let their joys be nourished,
Like a myrtle, ever green,
Owned by the Cyprian queen,
Who fosters it with rosy dew,
Where her nymphs their sport pursue.
Leave th' Aonian cave behind
(Come, O come with willing mind!)
And the Thespian rocks, whence drill
Aganippe waters still.
Chastest virgins, you that are
Either for to make or mar,
Make the air with Hymen ring,
Hymen, Hymenaeus sing!

2   *Ibid.*, p. 154.

CONCLUSION

It remains only to consider a few poets in whose work no trace of Catullus appears or, at best, only a very slight trace.

JAMES SHIRLEY (1596-1666) has, so far as I can discover, only one possible reference to Catullus, and that is, admittedly, a doubtful one.

(1)   From *Cupid's Call* (Gifford and Dyer, VI, p. 406):

Into Love's spring-garden walk;
Virgins dangle on their stalk,
Full blown and playing at fifteen;
Come, bring your amorous sickles then;
  See, they are pointing to their beds,
  And call to reap their maidenheads.

This simile may be drawn from *Carm.* lxii, 39-47:

Ut flos in saeptis secretus nascitur hortis,
Ignotus pecori, nullo convulsus aratro. . .
Sic virgo, dum intacta manet. . . .

HENRY GLAPTHORNE (1608-1643?) has one possible reference to Catullus:

(1)   From *To Lucinda, Upon the First Sight of her Beautie* (II, p. 171):

Those fools who sought to make
A star of Berenice's hair, might take
Hers for a planet, fix it, and ne'er fear
To dazzle Phoebus' lustre in the sphere.

Probably a reference to the *Coma Berenices, Carm.* lxvi.

In JOHN CLEVELAND (1613-1658) I can find no indication of any knowledge of Catullus. Though he wrote much in Catullus's satiric and coarser vein, the subjects which he dealt with, Presbyterianism and Fifth Monarchism and the like, were far different from the subjects of Catullus's venomous "iambics."

The little known GEORGE DANIEL of Beswick (1616-1657) sometimes falls into a strain reminiscent of Catullus. So in addressing his faithless mistress, he speaks with a touch of Catullus's mood and manner. Thus he declares in *To Sylvia Revolted* (Grosart, I, 48):

I will not wrong her name, which give mine life,
In a clear mention; she to whom I sung
A thousand sonnets, and brought numbers rife,
To celebrate her glories. . .

Later in *Sylvia Supplanted* (Grosart, I, 50,) he represents her as having fallen into the excesses of Lesbia:

Her limbs distorted, and her name profest,
Lewd prostitute to every stranger's call.

One phrase of his in this latter poem is distinctly Catullian:
> Split your proud heart with grief
> To know, another must
> Gain, by my verse, a life;
> While yours, lived *in the rust*
> Of sad decay, no mention shall find.

See *Carm.* lxviii, 149-152:
> Hoc tibi quod potui confectum carmine munus
> Pro multis, Alii, redditur officiis,
> Ne vestrum scabra tangat robigine nomen
> Haec atque illa dies atque alia atque alia.

The poems of JOSHUA SYLVESTER (1563-1618), of HENRY KING (1592-1669), of THOMAS STANLEY (1625-1678), and of AURELIAN TOWN-SHEND (1601-1643), if I may be permitted to group unlikes so arbitrarily, contain, so far as I can discover, no reference to Catullus.

In the secular poems of HENRY VAUGHAN (1621-1695), that is, in the *Olor Iscanus*, I have been able to find no indication of a knowledge of Catullus. In the religious poems, of course, there are none whatever.

BIBLIOGRAPHY

Addison, Joseph. *Miscellaneous Works* (ed. A. C. Guthkelch). London, 1914.

Bagguley, W. H. (ed.). *Andrew Marvell, Tercentenary Tributes*. Oxford, 1922.

Berdan, J. M. *Early Tudor Poetry*, 1485-1547. New York, 1920.

Brome, Alexander. *Poetry*. (Chalmers, English Poets, VI). London, 1810.

Browne, William. *Poems* (ed. Goodwin). London, 1894.

Cambridge History of English Literature, Volumes IV-VIII.

Campion, Thomas. *Works* (ed. Bullen). London, 1903.

Campion, Thomas. *Poetical Works in English* (ed. Vivian). London, N. D.

Carew, Thomas. *Poems* (ed. Vincent). London, 1889.

Carpenter, F. I. *English Lyric Poetry, 1500-1700*. London, 1897.

Cartwright, William. *Life and Poems* (ed. Goffin). Cambridge, 1918.

Case, R. H. *English Epithalamies*. London, 1896.

Castelain, M. *Ben Jonson, L' Homme et L'Oeuvre*. Paris, 1907.

Catullus. *Liber* (ed. Ellis). Oxford, 1867.

Catullus. *Poems* (ed. E. T. Merrill). Boston, 1893.

Catullus. *Poems of Gaius Valerius C.* (ed. Cornish). London, 1925.

Catulle. *Poesies* (ed. G. Lafaye). Paris, 1922.

Catullus. *Poems* (ed. Owen). London, 1893.

Catullus. *Carmina* (ed. Postgate). London, 1889.

Catullus. *Liber* (ed. Baehrens). 1893, 1895.

Catullus. *Carmina* (ed. Stuttaford). London, 1909.

Catullus. *Carmina* (ed. Doering). London, 1820.

Catullus. *Carmina* (ed. Gabbema). Zyll, 1659.

Chapman, George. *Minor Poems and Translations*. London, 1875.

Claudian. *Poetry* (ed. Platnauer). London, 1922.

Cleveland, John. *Poems* (ed. Berdan). New York, 1903.

Cowley, Abraham. *Poems* (ed. Waller). Cambridge, 1905.

Cowley, Abraham. *Essays, Plays, and Sundry Verses* (ed. Waller). Cambridge, 1906.

Cowley, Abraham. *The Mistress* (ed. Sparrow). London, 1926.

Crashaw, Richard. *English Poems* (ed. J. R. Tutin, Muses' Library). London, N. D.

Daniel, George. *Poems* (ed. Grosart). London, 1878.

Daniel, Samuel. *Poems* (Chalmers, English Poets, III). London, 1810.

Daniel, Samuel. *Delia*, with Drayton's *Idea* (ed. Esdaile). London, 1908.

Davies, Sir John. *Poems* (ed. Grosart). Edinburgh, 1878.

Donne, John. *Poetical Works* (ed. Grierson). Oxford, 1912.

Donne, John. *Poems* (ed. Chambers). London, 1896.

Donne, John. *Complete Poems* (ed. Grosart). London, 1872.

Drayton, Michael. *Poems* (Chalmers, English Poets, IV). London, 1810.

Drayton, Michael. *Minor Poems* (ed. Brett). Oxford, 1907.

Drummond, William. *Poems* (ed. Kastner). Manchester, 1913.

Drummond, William. *Poems* (ed. Ward). London, 1894.

Duckett, Eleanor S. *Catullus in English Poetry.* Northampton, 1925.

Dunlop, J. C. *History of Latin Literature to the Augustan Age.* London, 1825-28.

Dunn, Esther C. *Ben Jonson's Art.* Northampton, 1925.

Delattre, Floris. *Robert Herrick.* Paris, 1912.

Ellis, Robinson. *Commentary upon Catullus.* Oxford, 1876.

Erskine, John. *The Elizabethan Lyric.* New York, 1905.

Fellowes, E. H. *English Madrigal Verse.* Oxford, 1920.

Fletcher, Giles and Phineas. *Poetical Works* (ed. Boas). Cambridge, 1908.

Glapthorne, Henry. *The Poems and Plays.* London, 1874.

Gosse, Edmund. *The Life and Letters of John Donne.* London, 1899.

Gosse, Edmund. *Seventeenth Century Studies.* London, 1883.

Grierson, H. J. C. *The First Half of the Seventeenth Century.* London, 1906.

Grierson, H. J. C. *The Background of English Literature.* London, 1925.

Habington, William. *Castara* (ed. Elton). London, 1812.

Harrington, K. P. *Catullus and his Influence.* Boston, 1923.

Hartmann, C. H. *The Cavalier Spirit.* New York, 1925.

Herbert, George. *Poetical Works* (ed. Grosart). London, 1886.

Herford, C. H., and Simpson, Percy. *Ben Jonson,* Volumes I & II. Oxford, 1925.

Herrick, Robert. *Poetical Works* (ed. Moorman). Oxford, 1915.

Herrick, Robert. *Hesperides and Noble Numbers* (ed. Pollard). London, N. D.

Herrick, Robert. *Poetical Works* (ed. Grosart). London, 1876.

Johnson, Samuel. *Works: Lives of the Poets,* IX and X. London, 1823.

Jonson, Ben. *Complete Works* (ed. Gifford and Cunningham). London, 1875.

King, Henry. *The English Poems* (ed. Mason). London, 1914.

Lamb, G. L. *The Poems of Catullus Translated.* London, 1821.

Legouis, E. *A History of English Literature,* 650-1660. New York, 1926.

Lovelace, Richard. *The Poems of Lucasta* (ed. Phelps). Chicago, 1921.

Lowell, J. R. *Among My Books.* Boston, 1900.

Macdonagh, T. *Thomas Campion and the Art of English Poetry.* Dublin, 1913.

Martial. *Epigrammata* (ed. Ker). London, 1919.

Marvell, Andrew. *Poems* (ed. Aitken). London, N. D.

Masson, David. *Drummond of Hawthornden.* London, 1873.

Milton, John. *Poetical Works,* (ed. Masson). London, 1890.

Milton, John. *Prose Works* (ed. J. A. St. John). London, 1848.

Milton, John. *Areopagitica* (Arber Reprints). Westminster, 1895.

Moorman, F. W. *Robert Herrick, a Biographical and Critical Study.* London, 1910.

Morris, E. P. *An Interpretation of Catullus VIII.* 1909.

Mullinger, J. B. *Cambridge Characteristics in the Seventeenth Century.* London, 1867.

Munro, H. A. J. *Criticisms and Elucidations of Catullus.* Cambridge, 1878.

Newcastle, Margaret Duchess of. *Life of the First Duke of Newcastle.* New York, c. 1925.

Noël, F. *Notes sur les Poésies de Catulle.* Paris, 1803.

Ovid. *Tristia ex Ponto* (ed. Wheeler). London, 1924.

Palmer, Henrietta R. *List of English Editions and Translations of Greek and Latin Classics Printed before* 1641. London, 1911.

Pichon, René. *De Sermone Amatorio apud Latinos Elegiarum Scriptores*. Paris, 1902.

Propertius. *Poetry* (ed. Butler). London, 1922.

Quintilian, *Works* (ed. Gesner) Oxford, 1806.

Raleigh, Sir Walter. *Poems, with those of Sir Henry Wotton and other Courtly Poets, from* 1540-1650 (ed. Hannah). London, 189—.

Randolph, Thomas. *Complete Works* (ed. Hazlitt). London, 1875.

Randolph, Thomas. *Poems and Amyntas* (ed. Parry). New Haven, 1907.

Rhys, Ernest. *Lyric Poetry*. London, 1913.

Schelling, Felix E. *The English Lyric*. Boston, 1913.

Schelling, Felix E. *A Book of Seventeenth Century Lyrics*. Boston, 1899.

Schelling, Felix E. *English Literature During the Lifetime of Shakespeare*. New York, 1910.

Sherburne, Sir Edward. *Poems* (ed. Chalmers, English Poets, VI). London, 1810.

Shirley, James. *Works*, Vol. VI (ed. Gifford and Dyce). London, 1833.

Smith, G. G. *Ben Jonson*. London, 1919.

Stanley, Thomas. *Poems*, in *Caroline Poets*, III (ed. Saintsbury). Oxford, 1921.

Strode, William. *Poetical Works* (ed. Bobell). London, 1907.

Suckling, Sir John. *Works* (ed. Thompson). London, 1910.

Swinburne, A. C. *A Study of Ben Jonson*. London, 1889.

Townshend, Aurelian. *Poems and Masks* (ed. Chambers). Oxford, 1912.

Vaughan, Henry. *Works* (ed. Martin). London, 1914.

Waller, Edmund. *Poems* (ed. Drury). London, 1893.

Walton, Izaak. *Lives of Donne, Wotton, Hooker, Herbert, and Sanderson*. London, 1858.

Wendell, Barrett. *The Temper of the Seventeenth Century in English Literature*. New York, 1904.

Wilder, M. L. *Jonson's Indebtedness to Latin Authors, Shown Chiefly in his Non-Dramatic Poems*. Cornell University, 1926.

Wilder, M. L. *Did Jonson Write the Expostulation? Modern Language Review, XXI*

Wither, George. *The Poetry of George Wither* (ed. Frank Sidgwick). London, 1902.

INDEX